You Can Lead!

You Can Lead!

Discover Unusual Paths to Leadership

Katurah York Cooper

XULON PRESS

Xulon Press
2301 Lucien Way #415
Maitland, FL 32751
407.339.4217
www.xulonpress.com

Scripture quotations taken from the Holy Bible, New International
Version (NIV). Copyright © 1973, 1978, 1984, 2011 by Biblica,
Inc.™. Used by permission. All rights reserved.

Cover design by Sabina Banic Boakai
Cover photograph by Shoana Solomon

Printed in the United States of America.

ISBN-13: 9781545659182

For my mother
Louise Cordelia Wilson York
1925-2011
She lived the scripture "nothing is impossible with God"
and she taught me to believe its truth.

CONTENTS

Acknowledgements

I was asked to bring words of inspiration at a Praise Festival sponsored by the Gbowee Peace Foundation Africa on a Saturday morning during the Christmas Season. About one hundred Liberian women, ranging from 18-75 years old, were seated at tables laden with a sumptuous Liberian breakfast. A few minutes ago, they had been clapping and dancing to African drummers and the disc jockey's selection of favorite Liberian music. The air was permeated with goodwill, joy, and laughter. When it was time for me to speak, I stood before them with a few notes on a card. For fifteen minutes, I talked about living in a state of perpetual gratitude. Too many times we wait for a major event (marriage, graduation, moving into your own home, publishing a book) to have an elaborate thanksgiving ceremony. God shows us many small but significant events and people that come into our lives on any given day. That's why we need to be thankful every day!

One such small but significant event occurred when Candace Greene was the editor of the Empowerment

Temple-USA quarterly publication. While interviewing me for a story, she abruptly pressed the pause button on the voice recorder and said "Reverend Cooper, you have to write your story. Please write a book. Let me know if I can help in any way." On that day, she put aside her scripted questionnaire and invited me to tell my story uninterrupted with the recorder catching every word I spoke. I begin these acknowledgments with a big thank you to Candance. It's taken quite a number of years; and of course, the story has expanded. But I have always felt that if I didn't publish, Candance would be so disappointed. Here it is, the first of more books that are on the way.

I thank my mother in the ministry, Bishop Vashti Murphy McKenzie, who always makes it crystal clear that she expects nothing less than great things from me. She inspires me with her ability to rebrand herself in profound ways. I am grateful to Rev. Dr. Cecelia Williams Bryant who celebrates my every achievement and, in a subtle but meaningful way, spurred me on to complete this book.

Thank you to Dr. Richelle White, my dear friend who read the first draft manuscript and quelled my doubts when she said: "Girl, you are ready. Send it to the publishers!" I thank her for answering my many questions and helping me choose a publisher. Thank you to my hundreds of social media friends who kept reminding me that they are waiting for the book.

I am blessed to be the pastor of Empowerment Temple AME Church, Liberia. You have never questioned the various leadership paths I have embraced while serving as your pastor. My accomplishments are tied to you. Let's celebrate this book together.

I am grateful for the 'midwives' of this book, Reverend Musu Harris and Mother Belinda Yahwon. They brought together about forty Liberian women to celebrate my twenty-two (22) years in ministry and led them in raising funds; thereby providing the financial seed for the publication of this book.

You Can Lead! became a family project. I acknowledge the editorial critique offered by three of my daughters, Aisha, Jayme, and Kayonnoh. They were brutally honest while pushing me to go deeper in sharing my stories. Thanks to the rest of the team: Sowonee, Anna, Gbolahan, Marvin, James, Jandii, and Jaryee. You are the best, most supportive children in the universe.

My husband, James Cooper, is just amazing! Rather than slowing me down, he keeps pushing me forward to live my best, most fulfilled life. He has unflinching faith in my abilities, and he supported me through every challenge that came my way. Thank you for tolerating all the nights I slept cuddled with my computer. Your kind is rare.

I am also grateful to all those who shared their stories with me as well as the numerous unnamed persons I encountered in ministry in the United States and Liberia.

With humility, I acknowledge my total dependence on God who supplied all my needs for every step of this journey.

FOREWORD

*T*he devastation caused by the Liberian civil war is uncountable. Whilst many efforts have been placed on infrastructural rehabilitation and economic growth and development, very little has been done for filling the leadership gap needed for the continuous healthy transition of war-torn Liberia into a vibrant, prosperous nation. This leadership gap is partly the result of the perpetuation of an erroneous definition of authentic leadership as "leadership bestowed by privilege, training, authority, might or inheritance". Since there is really no such thing as a 'leadership gap', ill-equipped persons (without vision, passion nor calling), rise up and step into leadership positions. Because of this erroneous definition, many "invisible leaders" remain hidden, undiscovered, un-installed and the nation suffers.

The author is someone I have come to embrace as a pastor, a mentor and a friend. In addition, Reverend Katurah Cooper is a wife, mother, former refugee of the Liberian civil war, an educator and a peace advocate.

In this book, she interweaves her life stories with that of biblical characters, taking you on a fascinating journey of leadership self-discovery. I was captivated by the narrative of "The Wounded Leader". In that chapter, Reverend Cooper uses her story about the raw pains of marital betrayal (everything that women are taught in our society not to reveal in public), whilst attempting to do God's work and allowing God to take her through the strenuous process of healing. This healing process becomes one of the pathways leading to her leadership self-discovery.

You Can Lead! is revolutionary. Reverend Katurah Cooper shows every young woman that you can be whatever you want to be, regardless of your age and social status. At the same time, Reverend Cooper speaks to all, especially young men and women, who have been reluctant to see their leadership potential unfolding in the stories woven into the tapestry of their lives. On this powerful literary tour, this author offers ten poignant personal stories. She takes all of us on a robust, sometimes tragic but honest excursion of what could be a life which ends in unrealized potential; but, becomes a life of exhilarating, purposeful leadership.

Reverend Katurah Cooper teaches how a leader must celebrate achievements and milestones, mourn fears and failures but continue to strive for excellence. Over the years, I have found her life to be an inspiring example of a woman of unwavering faith, integrity and resilience. In a world where faith is persistently downplayed or used to create a sense of discomfort, this book uses faith in God to take us on a practical and relatable journey as we find ourselves in one or more of the ten leadership models. *You Can Lead!* is a simple but powerful affirmation. It is also insightful and inspiring.

Leymah Gbowee
Nobel Peace Prize Laureate (2011)
Founder, Gbowee Peace Foundation Africa

Introduction

The country of my birth, Liberia, announced her independence in 1847. Since then, Liberia has been on a sometimes hopeful, many times tortuous path in pursuit of national identity, political stability and economic self-reliance. It is indexed to be in the top five most impoverished countries in the world. Needless to say, we need leaders who can effect positive change.

Leadership is a microcosm of the culture of the larger society. Back in the 1970s, you could spot a Liberian leader by these distinct features. A leader was at least fifty years old, most likely a man, married with several children, and held a managerial position in an institution. He sat on the front row of the church every Sunday and was on one of the leadership boards. He was a member of either the Free Masonry or one of the other fraternal organizations. His wife and children catered to him and requested his approval and his consent to carry out the most mundane of tasks. He was the "king of the castle".

In the rural villages, the curriculum vitae of a typical leader read: fifty-year-old male, husband to three wives, speaks his tribal dialect excellently and English well-enough, owns a farm, has at least nine children, lives in his own house, could be a town or clan chief. His word is final in all things.

Postwar Liberia birthed a more dangerously distorted image of leadership. During the war, thousands of young people discovered the power of a gun. With a gun in hand, children as young as ten reduced fifty-year-old men and women to begging for their lives and that of their children. In the aftermath of the war, these children saw some of their rebel generals as well as their friends elevated to positions of leadership in Liberia. A warlord was voted in as a senator, compatriots with whom they shared looted goods became government ministers (i.e. Minister of Foreign Affairs). Leaders of marauding gang-rapists now became the 'honorables'. Those who stole vast sums of money from government coffers were given the best seats and the choicest positions. Fifteen years after the war ended, Liberians still go to the polls and elect persons who would typically be considered to be the least qualified to lead.

More recently, another image is emerging. If you are semi-literate, can mobilize and influence hundreds in your community behind an idea or cause, are constantly in the media on radio spewing out propaganda, and have some money to spend; then you are a leader.

In the preceding paragraphs, I have described models of leadership that have become common in my beloved nation. These models of leadership are not localized in Liberia (nor Africa) as many would have us believe.

Examples are scattered around the globe. In the past, these leadership models emerged as a result of coup d'états, or violent overthrow of elected heads of states. Recently, there is a global wave of leaders who are legitimately elected or installed; but, have neither the desire, expertise nor moral character to create a society of prosperity, respect, and progress in their nations. They are driven by the self-centered quest for personal wealth, and they rule with autocracy.

James MacGregor Burns suggests that leadership can take one of two forms—transactional leadership and transformational leadership. Transactional leadership occurs when leaders and followers operate in some type of exchange relationship in order to meet their needs. Transactional leadership, both common and transitory, exists when measurable mutual benefit occurs. Writing of Burns' contribution (36, 425-26), Hughes, Ginnet, and Curphy "also noted that while this type of leadership could be quite effective, it did not result in organizational or societal change and instead tended to perpetuate and legitimize the status quo" (632). Transformational leadership occurs when the status quo changes by appealing to followers' values and their sense of higher purpose.

In 1990, I along with my daughters fled the Liberian civil war and resided for eleven years in the United States. Despite the ongoing brutal civil war and compelled by the desire to serve my people; I returned to Liberia in 2001 to establish the Empowerment Temple AME Church. Three years later, Dr. Samuel Reeves, a pastor, and friend stopped by Empowerment Temple and sold me on to an idea to cofound the National Leadership Institute of Liberia. He argued that the only hope for war-ravished Liberia would be to focus on leadership training and development. We joined forces, invited other church leaders and began offering seminars in leadership development under the theme: "Lead Where You Are."

The Global Leadership Summit came to Liberia in 2010. It was then I was introduced to the critical importance of leadership development. I began to see all aspects of pastoral ministry through the lens of the principles of transformational leadership. I looked around my country, Liberia, and observed the administration of educational institutions, businesses, organizations, governments, and churches. What I discovered was alarming. Many heads of these entities as well as their followers were clueless of what real leadership is; hence giving truth to John Maxwell's axiom that "everything rises and falls on the leader". The fact is that our institutions are falling because of poor leadership.

You Can Lead! reminds me of driving through the Harbor tunnel during rush hour in Baltimore City. The lighting is not as good as sunlight, you feel claustrophobic, you are anxious to see the light at the exit, and you pray fervently that the car in front of you doesn't break down. *You Can Lead!* was in that tunnel for twelve years. Deborah's story was first written more than twelve years ago under the title "Lead Where You Are". It was eventually published in the AME Review. It was a single piece; and once submitted, I was done with it. Deborah's story would be like a seed scattered indiscriminately by the wayside that later germinates into a plant.

About three years ago I decided to explore publishing a book on leadership. *You Can Lead!* started as a quest to give commentary on leadership models in the bible. I went back and retrieved the article on Deborah. Following that same pattern, I selected other biblical characters and wrote an analysis of each of their stories. The intent was to help the reader find a connection with a biblical character's rise to leadership. As I wrote, flashes of my life story burst forth in my mind. I discovered points of connection with the life stories of those biblical characters.

I remembered a long-ago promise to publish my memoirs. Yet, I really wanted to write a book about leadership. In late 2017, I changed the style of the book. Moses' story was my wake-up call. Moses' life is protected because God has a major assignment for him. I thought of the three times my life was spared from a bullet. I thought about how, like Moses, I returned home to Liberia to lead a transformation of hundreds of clergy, women and young people. This eventually became the chapter titled: 'The Accidental Leader'.

Looking at the images of leadership carved out of my Liberian experience; I wondered about so many persons who have stayed at the fringes or hung in the back because they do not see themselves worthy or equipped to lead. I do not represent the typical patriarchal image of a Liberian leader. But that image has undergone a significant revision with the election of a woman, Ellen Johnson Sirleaf, as the first female head of state in Africa. Later she would be joined by Leymah Gbowee, a Liberian peace activist, to break another barrier: two female Nobel Peace Laureates from the same country honored in the same year. One of the poorest and least developed countries in the world has produced two female Nobel laureates and the first female national leader on the continent. Those events created a paradigm shift of tsunami proportions, and the ripple effects will continue to be felt for many years. How can we sustain this paradigm shift in leadership perception? How about all those potential leaders lurking in the shadows of society?

This book has a unique structure. Each chapter begins with an offering of one of ten of my personal stories. By connecting my stories to the stories of biblical characters, I navigate new terrains and chart unusual pathways to leadership. *You Can Lead!* is part memoir, part biblical commentary; however, it is intended for you to engage in journaling and self-discovery. It is meant to be interactive. Each chapter has a section on 'Lessons Learned' that will open up a world of possibilities for you as you are invited to reflect on your own life experiences. Each chapter ends with the question: "What's your story?". I urge every reader to write his/her own story. We are empowered by our own testimony. You may not have a relevant story to tell for every leadership path in the book, but you will have a story or two or more! I pray that as you read, you will discover one or more unique paths toward becoming the leader God has called you to be.

You Can Lead! may form part of your personal journaling, or it may be used in a team or group discussion forum. I have stories to share and so do you. The question is "what is your story and how is your story shaping your leadership development?".

Katurah York Cooper
January 2019

Chapter 1

The Accidental Leader

Exodus 3:10-11 "So now, Go. I am sending you to Pharaoh to bring the Israelites out of Egypt. But Moses said to God, "Who am I, that I should go to Pharaoh and bring the Israelites out of Egypt?"

Jeremiah 1:5 "Before I formed you in the womb I knew you. Before you were born, I set you apart. I appointed you as a prophet to the nations. (NRSV)

<u>My Story</u>

*T*hree times I have faced the threat of being killed by a bullet. In the early hours of April 12, 1980, 17 non-commissioned officers (NCOs) and soldiers of the Armed Forces of Liberia led by Master Sergeant Samuel Doe launched a bloody coup d'état. All of the conspirators were indigenous Liberians, while then-President William R. Tolbert was a member of the Americo-Liberian community. Americo-Liberian refers to citizens of Liberia who trace their immediate ancestors to free slaves who returned to live in Liberia during the early to mid 1800's. On the fateful morning, soldiers entered the Executive Mansion (presidential palace) and killed President Tolbert. His body was dumped into a mass grave together with twenty-seven other victims of the coup.

Later that same day armed men, posing as government soldiers, entered where I lived. At that time, my husband, Jim and I lived with his uncle while our home was under construction. His uncle was targeted and arrested because he worked for the Tolbert government as one of the deputy ministers. My husband was arrested along with this uncle. I stood and watched as they were shoved into the back of a pickup truck and driven away. I, my one-year-old daughter and a female relative were left with two soldiers who held us at gunpoint demanding money and jewelry from us. The two of us, young women in our 20s, were alone, frightened of the possibility of rape or death. I remember standing there with my first child in my arms, not knowing whether I would live or die. By the miracle of God's grace, the men turned and walked away leaving us in the house. All three of our lives were spared, and both of our male relatives returned to us unharmed that same day.

In December 1989, Charles Taylor, along with other Liberian rebels, invaded Liberia seeking to topple then President Samuel K. Doe regime. Taylor's actions began a civil war leaving more than 200,000 dead and one million refugees. My family was in the number of refugees who were scattered across the world. My husband stayed in Liberia while four of my daughters and I sought refuge in the United States of America in the city of Baltimore, Maryland. I had mixed feelings on that hot night in May as the girls, and I boarded the last flight out of Roberts International Airport. The decision to leave Liberia meant that we were not safe anymore. The last time I felt that way was April 6, 1980. I was grateful that we had the financial means to purchase five airplane tickets and the influence to get American visas for all of us. At least we would be safe in America until the war subsided when we could all go back home.

Six months after fleeing Liberia, I would be held at gunpoint for the second time. On November 1, 1990, I was standing in line at a bank in Baltimore enchasing a check when masked armed robbers entered. They had on Halloween masks so I thought this must be the left-overs from yesterday's trick and treaters. I was wrong. While one of them stood guard at the front door, the other two shouted at the three customers and bank employees commanding us to lay on the floor and be quiet. The robbers led the branch manager to the back of the building and proceeded to open the vault and loot it. As I lay there I thought *"Am I going to die today, after all, I went through to escape death in Liberia?"* I would hardly complete that thought when we noticed a burning smell in the hall. When the robbers were leaving, they had set a Molotov bottle in the center of the banking floor. I don't know why it did not explode. Instead, the carpet was burning. That was the source of the smell. When we realized the bank was on fire, we were in a state of panic. I vividly remember how we had to run out of the building to save our lives. For the second time, I survived.

In 1996, while the Liberian civil war was raging, a major attack drove my husband to flee from Liberia into Accra, Ghana and take refuge in that country. He had very limited financial resources. It became clear that it was time for him to leave Africa and join the family in Baltimore. We talked about getting an American visitor visa from the American embassy in Accra, but that would mean I had to travel from Baltimore to Accra to see him. I also needed a letter of support requesting for his visa. My pastor introduced me to Congressman Elijah Cummings of Baltimore, and the congressman provided that letter. I was on a quest to bring my husband back to America and unite our family. I also used that opportunity to take mission supplies to Liberian women residing in refugee camps in Ghana.

Four days after my arrival, at about 3 am, we were awakened by gunshots, windowpanes breaking and banging on the doors. Armed robbers were trying to enter the house. My husband pushed me out of bed and tried to force me under the bed. Imagine trying to squeeze under a bed and pull on a pair of jeans over nightclothes at the same time! The robbers entered and held us at gunpoint, demanding money, jewelry, and other valuables. I remember backing into the tiny bathroom behind me while mouthing the words "Jesus, Jesus, Jesus." One of the robbers said: "If you don't give us everything, we will kill your husband right before your eyes." Then they proceeded to ransack the entire room, screaming threats at us. Finally, they left with my briefcase containing all of my documents including airline tickets, and money. I was left with seven dollars. Though shaken and frightened, I survived for the third time. Unfortunately, my husband was denied the American visa. I returned to my children alone, downhearted and discouraged. Jim would return to Liberia seven months later while I continued to live peacefully in America for five more years until I received the call of God to return to Liberia.

Moses' Story

A baby boy was born to Jochebed and Amram at a time when having a 'boy child' was a curse. Without conscious knowledge, this baby was born when the Hebrew children were slaves of the Egyptians and living under harsh conditions of servitude. Exodus chapter 1 describes their ordeal-an entire nation of slave laborers, building the massive pyramids and architectural mansions of the Egyptians. Jehovah was silent as the suffering raged on for over 400 years. The pharaoh of Egypt was overwhelmed by the increase in the number of Hebrew births and felt intimidated by their increasing population. His response was to issue a decree which was a death sentence. It stated that all newborn Hebrew males should die and only female babies allowed to live.

To understand this act of the pharoah we have to deal with the value placed on male children over that of female children. As far back as Genesis, scripture appears to support this idea. God gives the responsibility of controlling the garden to Adam. (Gen. 3:9-11). After Adam and Eve had sinned; Eve is punished with these words "I will greatly increase your pangs in childbearing; in pain, you shall bring forth children, yet your desire shall be for your husband, and he shall rule over you." (Gen.3:16). The daughters of Zelophehad had no rights of inheritance to their father's property because he had no sons and the law forbid women to own property. (Num. 27: 1-10). The phenomenon of the "first-born son" is an important social construct of the Jewish family. Isaac's first-born Esau, though entitled to double inheritance and the birth-right, would lose it to Jacob in exchange for food. (Gen. 25:29-34, 27:1-4). Throughout scripture, we do not find any mention of special rights and privileges of a "first-born daughter."

Therefore, in a society where the announcement "It's a boy!" is greeted with shouts of jubilation; the pharoah's decree would leave Jochebed in tears when her baby boy emerged after painful labor. What a strange twist of circumstances! In defiance of the pharaoh's decree, the Hebrew midwives, Shiphrah and Puah, looked down at the beautiful baby boy and decided to let this boy live. Fearing Jehovah, they quietly laid the baby at Jochebed's breast and left the family to figure out how to protect their newborn son. The room was filled with joy and pain. The atmosphere was charged with anxiety, fear, and despair as Jochebed realized that the Egyptians would soon seize her child and drown him in the Nile River.

On that fateful day, Jochebed looked with love and anguish at her baby boy and decided "This one will live!". It is noteworthy that her determination to protect her child from certain death was not based on a heavenly visitation with a prophecy about her son. Amazingly

1. There was no prophetic announcement or prophetic conception.
2. There was no call for the family to make preparations for this baby boy's arrival.
3. There was no divine outline of plans for this baby boy.
4. There was no special name given to this baby boy forecasting his future.

The courage of this loving mother birthed the fight for this child's life. There was something special about this boy child! Verse 1 of Exodus 2 describes it well. "And a man of the house of Levi went and took as wife a daughter of Levi. So the woman conceived and bore a son. And when she saw that he was a beautiful child, she hid him three months."

What unfolds is a fascinating story of Jochebed weaving a beautiful basket, lining it with tar and placing her son in it. She and her daughter, Miriam, took the baby down to the river and set the basket with the baby among the reeds in the river. Miriam sat among the grasses watching and protecting the basket from floating far down the river. Along comes the pharaoh's daughter for a swim and sees the baby boy. Unable to ignore his loveliness and compelled by compassion; she rescues the baby and adopts him as her child. Big sister Miriam comes forward out of the reeds and offers to find a wet-nurse for the child. The pharoah's daughter names him Moses which means 'drawn out of the water.' Jochebed is hired as his wet-nurse, and Moses is safe, protected and begins his life as the grandson of the very man who decreed his death! (Exodus 2:7-10.)

Moses comes of age to his heritage as a Hebrew when he comes upon an Egyptian beating one of his kins-folk. (Exodus 2:11-20). With a sense of righteous anger, Moses kills the Egyptian and buries him. The next day, he comes upon two Hebrews fighting and admonishes them for this behavior. He is rebuked by these words "Who made you a ruler and judge over us? Do you mean to kill me as you killed the Egyptian?" (verse 14a). Fearing for his life, Moses flees Egypt and eventually begins a new life in Midian, meets the man Jethro and marries his daughter, Zipporah.

It is eighty years later when Moses, a shepherd, and father living in Midian, gets a heavenly visitation at the burning bush. Exodus chapter 3 records that encounter. Yahweh commands Moses to go back to Egypt and lead the march of the Hebrew slaves out of Egypt and into freedom. What ensues is a battle of will. Moses argues against going back while God insists that he must go back. Moses finally obeys and returns to Egypt to serve his people.

Lessons Learned

At God's set time, Moses finally understood that nothing happened in his life by accident. The pharaoh's daughter saved his life so that he could preserve his peo-ple's lives. He grew up in the palace to learn the ways of the pharaohs and return to challenge the pharaoh. Living as a refugee created a yearning for his people back in

Egypt. Faced with the reality of his life purpose at the burning bush, Moses began to stutter and doubt whether he could carry out this assignment. However, it became clear that God provided refugee status for him for the future execution of a divine mission.

For some time, I pondered over the miracle of protection over my life. My husband spent all the war years in Liberia, yet he was held at gunpoint only once in spite of the constant threats of bullets and mortar rockets propelled across the city. The dead and mutilated bodies all over the city streets attest to the fact that the war was indeed deadly. I escaped the war zone, yet I was not spared the repeated trauma brought on by my near-death experiences. Like Moses, I ran for refuge to a distant land; yet I could not run from God's call to go back to my people.

In August of 2018, I was the guest of the Liberian Ambassador to the United States of America, Counselor Lois Lewis Brutus. As I sat across the table and enjoyed the deliciously-prepared food and the gracious hospitality of the Embassy staff; I began to reflect on the life of Ambassador Brutus. I wondered if she ever dreamed that she would occupy the #1 diplomatic position in Liberia. I was sitting with a woman who was captured by rebel forces in 1995 and held for five days in rural Lofa County with no food, little water and the daily threat of rape and death. At that time, did she imagine herself a top diplomat in 2018? Ambassador Brutus, shared that, back in 1995, there was only one constant, pervasive thought and that was 'would we live to see another day?'

By God's grace, she was rescued. She fled the country but felt compelled to return from exile to do something for her people. She became the organizing President of the Association of Female Lawyers of Liberia (AFEL). That organization still exists today and is recognized for landmark work in crafting the Rape Bill in Liberia, the Property Rights for Widows and the subsequent advocacy that led to the passage of both bills into law.

Lois and I survived the danger of guns and war. You may have lived through the danger of cancer, HIV AIDS, childhood physical and emotional abuse, mental illness, gender-based violence, attempted suicide and abject poverty. Each of these is life-threatening and traumatic. You look at yourself today and realize that you survived somehow. It is sobering to think that God will preserve your life even when you don't have a clear understanding of God's purpose.

Accidental leaders are born to lead and do not know it. They are unaware that their lives are being shaped and protected for leadership. Accidental leaders are not aware that

1. God always has a plan for a people's deliverance, and it involves the birth of a leader.
2. The birth and life of that leader is frequently under attack and imminent threat of death.
3. God puts people in place to protect the leader.
4. God puts people in the position to provide for the leader.
5. God creates a wilderness experience for the leader.
6. God keeps the leader linked to the people.

<u>Reflection & Response</u>

Are you an accidental leader? Take a few minutes to do the following:

1. Reflect on the circumstances of your birth and threats to your life
2. Reflect on the divine provision, protection, times of separation from your people
3. Reflect on your natural judgment choices: standing up for a cause or an injustice
4. Reflect on your wilderness experience: going through times of adversity and scarcity of resources
5. Reflect on your calling: an unexpected encounter with God

Trace the trajectory of your life and ask yourself: Could it be possible that I am born for this daring leadership task and did not realize it? What an amazing possibility!

<u>What's Your Story?</u>

Journal

_____
_____
_____
_____
_____
_____
_____
_____
_____
_____
_____
_____
_____
_____
_____
_____
_____
_____
_____
_____
_____
_____
_____
_____
_____
_____
_____
_____

Chapter 2

The Un-Commissioned Leader

Judges Chapters 4 & 5

Judges 5: 7 & 12a "The peasantry prospered in Israel, they grew fat on plunder, because you arose, Deborah, arose as a mother in Israel. Awake, awake, Deborah! Awake, awake, utter a song!.." (NRSV)

<u>My Story</u>

*W*hile a refugee in America, my daughters and I tried to find a suitable church home. After visiting several African Methodist Episcopal (AME) Churches, we found a home at Payne Memorial AME Church where a dynamic female pastor, Reverend (now Bishop) Vashti Murphy McKenzie, had just been appointed. This church is located in a predominantly black downtown Baltimore area. It was the right fit because the children quickly made friends and got immersed in a youth ministry that catered to their spiritual and emotional needs. I became friends with women who I still consider my best friends more than twenty-five years later. Reverend McKenzie was an excellent mentor, and she quickly recognized my gifts; giving me an opportunity to serve as a Trustee Board member. What did not change was that I was a refugee, uprooted from my place of status in the Liberian society. My primary focus was on adjusting to this new life and making sure my family survived. I began teaching part-time at Morgan State University and serving at my local church. It quickly became apparent that God was moving me in the direction of church leadership; however, my hope and prayers were for the Liberian civil war to end. Months before I acknowledged the call to leadership as a call to preach; I found myself in a place of confusion and restless energy. Life didn't make sense. I would cry out to God asking the question: "What am I supposed to do with my life now that I am a refugee in America?".

On February 6, 1995, I embarked on solitary confine-ment with the Holy Spirit. I checked into a hotel with Bible and notepad and wrestled as Jacob wrestled with the angel (Genesis 32:22-32). I desperately needed God to give me a sense of direction. Twenty-four hours later I left that room convicted of my call to the preaching min-istry and the vision of the Miracle Women Workshops (MWW). This ministry would serve the women of Payne Memorial AME Church as a safe-space for them to share their struggles, develop an intimate relationship with the Lord and find solutions to their problems.

I did not leave the hotel and go straight to my pastor. I was scared and unsure of my abilities. I bargained with God. I would tell my pastor about the MWW but not about the call to preach. I love to analyze everything, so I argued to myself: *"I am just an ordinary church member with no credentials for ministry. I have not attended any ministry training classes"*. I remember struggling to convince myself that this whole idea would be accepted. Finally, I wrote the vision down and presented it to my pastor. To my surprise, she agreed to the plan and told me to move forward and put together a team. This was unprecedented. I was permitted to lead without conferral of a title or a ministry position! Let me quickly say that I received opposition from some of the leadership of the Women Missionary Society (WMS) of the church. They saw this new ministry as unnecessary since there was already a WMS in place. They questioned my credentials and whether I was adequately prepared to lead a woman's group since I had been born and raised in Africa. How could I possibly possess the skills and knowledge to lead in an American context? This attitude stemmed from a lack of understanding of my background and the false idea that being from the continent of Africa labels one as inferior. Nevertheless, I pressed on, the MWW grew and thrived for five years.

Deborah's Story

The legendary Deborah, the wife of Lappidoth, prophetess, and judge, is a beautiful, fantastic example of an empowered woman considering the extremely patriarchal

15

society of her time. The scripture records that fifteen judges ruled Israel. Deborah is listed as the only female judge in the Bible during an era when Israel had kings. It was a difficult time in Israel's history. Jabin, the king of Hazor, had subjected Israel to 20 years of oppression. A well-trained commander named Sisera led Jabin's army. Sisera controlled nine hundred chariots and a mighty army while the Israelites had no military strength. How amazing that a woman was a Judge of Israel during such a difficult time? The writer of Judges does not mince words when he states in Judges 4:4 that Deborah was leading Israel at that time.

In Judges 4: 6-7, Prophetess Judge Deborah receives divine instructions to send for a man named Barak. When he arrives, she informs him that he has been chosen to lead the deliverance of Israel from King Jabin, the Canaanite. An interesting thing happens. Barak, whether fearful or intimidated, insists that Deborah stand by his side throughout his military assignment. Listen to his words "If you go with me, I will go; but if you don't go with me, I won't go" (Judges 4:8). Deborah agrees to go with Barak and stand shoulder to shoulder with him. Her popularity and influence would be vital in encouraging the troops to fight valiantly. We see her right there when the attack campaign begins. Barak was the one with the title and position of Commander of the army. Deborah would be the one with the power that influenced the successful outcome.

<u>Lessons Learned</u>

Deborah was a leader but, she was not a military leader. Judge Deborah was not trained in battle and combat strategy. Therefore, she gladly obeyed the command of God to send for Barak and inform him that God had chosen him to be the Commander in charge of the army that would defeat Sisera's 900 chariot army. We must take note of two startling developments. Within the context of Israel's patriarchal society, the fact that Barak responded when Deborah summoned him is a testimony to her power and respect. Secondly, the fact that Barak insisted that she accompany him on the battlefield is a testimony to her influence and expertise. Can you imagine the reaction of other fighting men when they observed Barak elevate a woman to such a position? They probably argued that this woman was not equipped to fight just like the WMS doubted that I was qualified to lead the women of the church. Too many times, we use the popular formula of our times to discount and exclude classes of people from certain positions of authority.

I met Mrs. Ruth Sando Perry in the 1980s when she worked as a bank teller in one of Liberia's prominent banks. She was also my neighbor. Her home was just three doors down from mine. Her story is typical of a Liberian girl. Born in a rural setting to indigenous Liberian parents; she enrolled at a mission school established by the Episcopalian church. After high school, she got married and went on to have six children. Her husband entered politics and won a seat in Congress. His unexpected death changed the trajectory of Mrs. Perry's life.

She decided to contest for his vacant seat in the Senate. Despite criticism, discouragement and little political party support; she won and became a senator. She thought this was the pinnacle of her life and she marveled at her accomplishment. Looking back, this was the preparation for a much bigger leadership assignment.

In 1990, Liberia was engaged in a brutal civil war. As the battle raged on year after year, several attempts at brokering peace and ending the war would fail. However, for Ruth Sando Perry, that war would be the launching pad for her rise to historical leadership in Liberia.

In 1996, while attending an ECOWAS (Economic Community of West African States) Peace Conference on Liberia, she was summoned to appear before the six military heads of the warring factions and officials of ECOWAS. In her own words, she gives this account: "These six men asked if I would consent to be the Head of State of Liberia and Chairwoman for the Council of State [which would include all six men]. I asked them why they had selected me? They said because 'you are the only one we can trust and because we see you as a mother, a reconciler, and a neutral person.'" As Chair of the Council of State, Her Excellency Mrs. Ruth Sando Perry would successfully broker a cease-fire among the six warlords, oversee the disarmament of fighters and facilitate the conduct of elections in 1997. The impact of her less than two-year rule would significantly influence the election in 2005 of Mrs. Ellen Johnson Sirleaf as the first democratically elected female head of state in Africa.

Deborah, without commission nor title, stepped up and said yes to the call to lead in the fight. Deborah understood that when God speaks, you obey! God's people had to be set free. She realized that she was called upon to fill a gap. She was compelled to serve where seemingly she was not trained to function effectively. Like Deborah, Ruth Sando Perry and I were already leading but in areas that were far removed from our ultimate destiny. I was a university professor and a businesswoman; knowing nothing about leading in a ministry setting, and Ruth was a bank employee, former Senator knowing nothing about leading a nation. Barak told Deborah that he could not fight Jabin's army without her and those six warlords told Ruth Perry that they could not reconcile without her.

While Judge Deborah and Senator Ruth Perry did not hesitate to accept the call; it took me four months to finally step up to the assignment. Many of you are probably like me; hesitant to say yes to God. Looking back, I can only marvel at how we can become so impressed with titles that we refuse to forge ahead and fulfill a God-ordained vision. We want letters of accreditation and certificates of appointment. I have learned that God is not impressed with titles. God is looking for obedience.

Here are some important things to remember:

- We don't always receive letters of appointment or commission as the head
- We don't get to choose our platform for leadership
- We must decide to lead no matter our title or position or credentials

To be a leader of integrity is to order your life in the assurance that God does not make a mistake. God knows the exact person needed for specific tasks. We must stand up and quickly move to do what needs to be done. God has the master plan.

Reflection & Response

Have you ever hesitated to step forward because a title has not been conferred on you?

Have you ever been overlooked, set aside, side-lined, stepped on, pushed over, credentials down-played, accomplishments disrespected, yet God keeps affirming the call to leadership on your life?

Imagine the consequences

- If Deborah had refused to step up to lead because God did not give the title of "Commander" to her but rather to Barak?
- If Deborah had taken a stubborn, disobedient posture
- If Deborah had refused to be a team player
- If Deborah had been jealous of Barak's title

Now think about your life and wonder if your destiny goals are aborted because you are waiting to lead from a titled position. Ask yourself.

Is my nation's deliverance being held up?
Is my community's rebirth being killed?

Is my family's prosperity being delayed?
Is my destiny being stalled?

You may be an un-commissioned leader; yet, God is commanding you to rise up now! God wants you to lead from the side, the back, below or wherever. You need to stand up and lead just where you are!!

<u>What's Your Story?</u>

Journal

Chapter 3

ESTHER:
The Reluctant Leader

The Book of Esther

Esther 4:14 "For if you remain silent at this time, relief and deliverance for the Jews will arise from another place, but you and your father's family will perish. And who knows but that you have come to your royal position for such a time as this?"(NIV)

<u>My Story</u>

*B*ack in the early 1990s, I was comfortably residing in the United States of America far from the raging war in Liberia. I knew of the terrible times in Liberia. BBC, CNN and the stories from refugees reached my eyes and ears; but, all I wanted was to forget about the devastation going on at home. I was tired hearing the horrifying stories and receiving the sympathetic sentiments from church members and co-workers. I fixed my priority on taking care of my girls and making sure they had the best life under those circumstances. Jim, my husband, and I were blessed. We had some savings because of the Employee Provident Retirement Scheme of the Liberia Bank for Development & Investment. Jim was the General Manager of that bank when the war broke out. In late 1990, we received terrible news from home. The current president of the bank was killed in an ambush. At that time, Jim was in America contemplating whether to leave Liberia permanently or return to Liberia when the fighting subsided. Upon the murder of the bank's President, the bank's shareholders prevailed on Jim to go back to Liberia and take the position of president to secure the operation of the bank. We wrestled with that proposal. Ultimately, we decided that he would return to Liberia.

Meanwhile, the children and I remained in America taking residence in a pleasant suburban neighborhood. The children enrolled in good public schools. In time, my Liberian identity became dulled by the lure of the western world, and I began to think and make decisions from that worldview. Nevertheless, I suffered through periods of depression. When I became depressed from the terrible war news from Liberia; I went shopping with whatever funds I could gather. You do not have to be a millionaire to buy a 'lot of things,' and so I did just that; running up credit cards along the way. Looking back, I think there ought to be a tutorial for immigrant families to warn them about the trap of "shopping." The retail system in America quickly sucks you into debt. Stores with their shiny, beautiful things intoxicated me and numbed my feelings of despair and promptly dried up my lonely tears. I made peace with my situation and assimilated into the American lifestyle of materialism. Though I was unsettled in my spirit and knew this was not the life I wanted, yet; I was comfortable. I had a wonderful sisterhood at Payne Memorial AME Church in Baltimore. I established and ran a successful business called African Accents. Comfort did not mean perfect or the best. Comfort, for me, meant I had accepted my predictable life in America, I had my children with me, and I had wonderful friends. Comfort meant that my children and I were safe. My children were well-cared for, and we lived like middle-class America.

However, after the third year, we had no savings left; a large amount had been spent on paying for the travel of family members out of Liberia into safety in other countries. We began to lose hope of returning to Liberia in the near future. Instead of ending, the war had escalated, and Liberians were leaving the country for refugee camps or whichever country would accept them. Soon our family would be dealt a terrible blow. In 1995, my husband was forced out of his position as bank president because of political pressure from the ruling government. This left us without a viable source of income, and I realized that I had used vital finances to comfort myself and to appease the children with material things. Now, God had my full attention. My journey to answering the call to ministry began. Central to my call to ministry was God's desire to dismantle my false sense of comfort.

Discomfort is the fertile ground for God to plant the seed of ministry. I woke up from the "American Dream" to the reality that God was calling me out of my comfort zone to preach the gospel. Less than a year later, God spoke to my heart to travel to the refugee camps in Ghana and take 'Love Batons' to the women there. A Love Baton is a large tube mailer stuffed with travel size toiletries and personal items. I asked for donations of toiletries commonly available in hotel rooms and used during travel. My first venture out of my comfort zone was a trip to Ghana in 1996. I traveled to the Sanzule Refugee camp with these Love Batons. There I met with about eighty Liberian women living under refugee tents with not much more than the clothes on their backs. I hosted the Miracle Women Workshop there, and that was the seed for the establishment of the Miracle Women Worldwide Ministry.

By this time my journey to ordained ministry had begun. I became a licentiate in 1995, and I enrolled in the Masters of Divinity program at Wesley Theological Seminary in 1998. I graduated in May 2001; and in that same year, I was ordained itinerant elder by the Baltimore Annual Conference. In that same year, I was compelled by the Holy Spirit to leave America and return to Liberia to serve my people. This was the final demise of the comfort zone I had erected in the United States of America. In August, I left Maryland, USA and established The Empowerment Temple African Methodist Episcopal Church in Monrovia, Liberia. I left my home of eleven years. I left my five daughters, and I returned to Liberia where I still live and minister.

Esther's Story

Esther is an undercover Jewish maiden who rises to be Queen in the land of Persia. Her uncle Mordecai, confident of Esther's beauty and intelligence and determined to create a better life for his orphaned niece; allows her to enter a beauty contest that would lead to her selection as the next Queen of Persia. Mordecai warns her to keep her true identity a secret even changing her name from Haddasah to Esther. Queen Esther is loved, pampered, showered with every beautiful thing her heart desires. Life is good. Life is comfortable, and she loves every minute of it.

What appears to be a perfect life is about to be shattered. Haman, a trusted servant of the king, was promoted to the rank of vizier, a position above all the other princes. He was influential to the extent that all of the king's servants bowed down and paid homage to him. "But Mordecai (Esther's uncle) would not bow or pay homage (Esther 3:2). This so angered Haman that he convinced the king to make a decree for the execution of the Jews because "their laws are different from all other people's and they do not keep the king's laws" (Esther 3:8-9).

Upon hearing this, Mordecai becomes distressed with the horrible thought that an entire nation was about to be destroyed. He turns to Queen Esther for help insisting that she goes to the king to convince him to revoke the decree. Imagine her dilemma! Unless the king sent for you, no wife dared seek an audience with him. This was the law.

As the dialogue unfolds, an exasperated Mordecai insists that Esther is well-positioned to devise a plan to stop this plot. Of course, she refuses; for, to agree would mean to disturb the beautiful life she has. Mordecai was asking her to risk everything. Finally, she agrees. Her first act is to seek spiritual courage, so she calls for all the Jews and her maidens to join her in a fast. The second act is to skillfully develop and execute a plan to get the King to reverse his deadly decree. Queen Esther is granted an audience with the king. She prepares two nights of feasting, and through skillful manipulation and with divine intervention, Haman's plot is exposed. The king orders the hanging of Haman. The Jews are spared, and Mordecai (a Jew) is elevated to a position second to King Ahasuerus, King of Persia.

Lessons Learned

Queen Esther's story is in some ways my story. In Queen Esther's case, she was living a life of privilege and wealth; her every need attended to. I was definitely one of the privileged Liberian children. From birth, I had loving parents, adequate daily meals, a family car to take me to school. My father would say: "Your job is simple: go to school, study hard, be obedient and bring home good grades." Queen Esther was living the good life. No wonder she rejected the suggestions from Uncle Mordecai. What he wanted could threaten her comfortable situation! I can understand the reluctance of Queen Esther to jeopardize her choice position in life. It is easy to build a cocoon of false security around you when the outside world looks scary and uncertain. Survival and self-preservation are instinctive.

The very first sermon I preached back in 1995 was titled "The Danger of Living in the Comfort Zone." The fact is a comfort zone is a place of complacency due to anesthesia which numbs your awareness of suffering and pain. Queen Esther, like me, was living in that zone while masquerading in a lifestyle of prosperity and fulfillment. We were citizens of a foreign land. Esther was an under-cover Jew married to a Persian King, and I was a Liberian refugee acting like an American citizen.

It took a great leap of faith for Queen Esther to risk her comfortable place of privilege to save her people. Hers is an incredible story of courage, sexual intrigue, and political cunny. Set in an atmosphere of delectable food and intoxicating wine, Esther showcased the power of beauty, brains, and faith. Queen Esther also teaches us the significance of right timing. In Ecclesiastes chapter 3, we read that there is a time and a season for everything.

Just before my ordination in May of 2001, I was warned that there were no openings for new pastors in the Baltimore Annual Conference. Sixty itinerant elders were waiting for a pastoral assignment. Given my gifts and pas-sion for ministry, I started exploring opportunities in the United Methodist Church. I debated taking off two years from the AME Church to serve as a pastor in the United Methodist Church. My one-year internship at Asbury United Methodist in Washington, DC, won me a strong recom-mendation from the pastor. I was offered a pastoral charge in one of the smaller UM churches; however, it somehow never materialized. I am convinced that God wanted me to leave the United States entirely. I had to get away from the American life. The Holy Spirit pushed me to take a leap of faith into war-ravaged Liberia. The critical decision was made, and I chose to leave my comfort zone. Leadership requires courage: the courage to put yourself on the line, the courage to venture into scary, unknown territory, the courage to seize the opportunity and to do the right thing at the right time, the courage to walk on water.

Reflection and Response

Nowadays, change is a popular word that invokes both positive and negative feelings. Many would prefer to remain where they are, secure in the fact that they are coping well with their circumstances. We need to consider that

1. Change is part of life. We must expect our conditions to change.
2. Don't become too attached to your comfortable lifestyle. Wear it like clothing and not like skin.
3. If you don't take risks, you will miss out on God's divine assignment.
4. Discomfort is the mother of ministry.

Think about how you have resisted the call to do something about a situation because to act would disturb your comfort zone? Many leaders are birthed out of the need to fulfill an assignment. What about you? Winston Churchill puts it like this: "There comes a special moment in everyone's life, a moment for which that person was born. That special opportunity, when he seizes it, will fulfill his mission—a mission for which he is uniquely qualified. At that moment, he finds greatness. It is his finest hour."

What's Your Story?

Journal

_____

_____

_____

_____

_____

_____

_____

_____

_____

_____

_____

_____

_____

_____

_____

_____

_____

_____

_____

_____

_____

_____

_____

_____

_____

Chapter 4

The Wounded Leader

II Corinthians 12: 7 & 10: "And lest I should be exalted above measure through the abundance of the revelations, there was given to me a thorn in the flesh, the messenger of Satan to buffet me, lest I should be exalted above measure." "Therefore, I take pleasure in infirmities, in reproaches, in needs, in persecutions, in distresses, for Christ's sake. For when I am weak, then I am strong."

<u>My Story</u>

War is a very terrible thing! There are financial, social, human and spiritual casualties that occur. One of the significant casualties of the Liberian civil war was the breakdown of marriages and separation of family members. In early 1990, as the fighting forces advanced on the capital city of Monrovia; many wives and children fled the country while the husbands stayed behind to monitor the situation and protect the family properties. In May 1990, our daughters and I boarded the last flight out of Roberts International Airport (Monrovia) landing in Brooklyn, New York. Jim, my husband, would remain in Liberia throughout the eleven years of my stay in America. During that time, Jim visited us once a year, but at one point we did not see him for over fifteen months. We were even luckier than other families. Many Liberian wives did not see their husbands for five to ten years. The wives struggled to raise the children in America or somewhere in the diaspora while the husbands struggled to manage life in the midst of war.

I had always prided myself on what others called "our perfect marriage." Jim and I fell in love in high school. I was fifteen, and he was eighteen; young, but we were serious about our relationship. We had been married for almost thirteen years when the civil war started. Looking back, I realize that even before the civil war our marriage was showing signs of a struggle. The newly-wed euphoria was wearing off. We seemed to be moving apart, and there was a restlessness brewing that neither of us understood. Then we became separated by war! The abrupt separation, intensified by living on two different continents, deepened the cracks in our marriage. What I have described was the story for many Liberian marriages.

This situation created the environment for extra-marital relationships (both husbands and wives). This state of affairs became the order of the day creating feelings of guilt, distrust, anger, and frustration. Of course, marriages suffered. Our marriage was not exempt from this experience. During my years of exile, my husband began an extramarital relationship in Liberia. We had to deal with this situation, and the prospect of divorce was a strong option. It took God's grace, several interventions and the wisdom of some elders of our family to get us to the decision to give our marriage a second chance. In the year 2000, we began the long, painful process of restoring our marriage.

I left Baltimore, Maryland in 2001 and returned to Liberia to establish a church and to begin my first pastoring experience. At the same time, I started a new chapter in my life as a mother to an infant child from my husband's extramarital relationship. At that time, my youngest child was sixteen years old and about to graduate from high school. I was through with raising children. Jim and I were in our forty's and in good health. After so many years of forced separation, I desperately wanted to bask in the loving attention of my husband again. I dreamed of an endless honeymoon (without children everywhere). Instead, I was about to begin the task of parenting an 18-month old child. I was not forced into that decision. Jim and I decided that it would be the best path to follow and we have no regrets. Our 18-month old daughter is now eighteen years old and a freshman in college. She has a beautiful, loving and healthy relationship; not only with me but with all of her siblings. She is my daughter, and I am her mama. I have yet to fully comprehend the process and find the right words to describe all of the emotions: fear, joy, pain, hope, frustration, courage, anger; as well as the profound sacrifices and depth of love that it took to get us to this beautiful place.

All of this is happening just as I begin my new ministry era in Liberia at a time of complexity and confliction. Let me try to describe it.

I. I returned with a passion and a vision for ministry at a time when the war was still on, and the social/moral fabric of our society was in shambles.

II. I returned at a time that young Liberian women were starving for older women to serve as role models and a moral compass for them.

III. Sexual promiscuity, infidelities, violence in marriages, child marriages, prostitution, rape were norms, and the war had torn away all society's checks and balances against such behaviors.

IV. I was ministering to a congregation of depressed, war-weary, sad, poor people with little hope of ever living in peace.

Daily, I wrestled with the blatant testimony of our marital failures. I was angry and my anger was directed against my husband and the woman in the relationship. I was torn between feelings of distrust and hope. I became judgmental and kept pushing Jim to repent, pray more and act more 'spiritual'. I was tormented with the perception that others were judging us. I imagined the criticism of the congregation as I mounted the pulpit to preach Sunday after Sunday.

Such was the condition of my personal life for about five years. The thorns were in my flesh, and they would not leave me in peace. I must admit that the most painful thorns were the ones I inflicted on myself. They were the thorns of my judgmental attitude, my fears, my unhappiness, my insecurities, my distrust. While it is true that the healing had begun, the pain of the thorns remained for a long time. I would cry to the Lord and ask for relief. There were Sunday mornings when I did not feel like standing before the congregation because all I wanted was for the emotional pain to go away. Surprisingly, the ministry was growing, church membership increasing, lives were being transformed, and I remained faithful to the call of God on my life.

<u>Paul's Story</u>

Paul was formerly known as Saul, chief persecutor of the followers of Jesus Christ. While in hot pursuit of Christ's followers; he had a spiritual awakening encountering Jesus on the Damascus road (Acts 9). This conversion experience changed his life forever. He was given a new name, Paul, and embarked on an evangelistic mission to the Gentiles; establishing churches throughout Asia Minor and Europe.

Paul writes to the Corinthian church of how he had a divine revelation of great significance. These revelations would come in a vision and would reveal the extent to which Paul would excel in ministry. Paul describes it as a remarkable revelation! Paul would be chosen by God to be used mightily in saving souls. The impact of his ministry would be extensive. Paul writes about being tempted to boast of this; like others who had boasted of performing miracles, healings and deliverance. But, alas, this great man of God would share with us his 'thorn' in this flesh.

Listen to Paul: "And lest I should be exalted above mea-sure through the abundance of the revelations, there was given to me a thorn in the flesh, the messenger of Satan to buffet me, lest I should be exalted above measure."(II Corinthians 12:7). Scripture does not explain nor describe Paul's thorn, but we know that it was real and that it was a constant reminder of his need for God's grace.

Paul is considered the greatest apostle. His epistles to the churches make up the majority of the New Testament. Paul would be faithful to the end. Paul gives his testimony recorded in 2 Corinthians 11: 24-28.

"Five times I received from the Jews the forty lashes minus one. Three times I was beaten with rods, once I was pelted with stones, three times I was shipwrecked, I spent a night and a day in the open sea. I have been constantly on the move. I have been in danger from rivers, in danger from bandits, in danger from my fellow Jews, in danger from Gentiles; in danger in the city, in danger in the country, in danger at sea; and in danger from false believers. I have labored and toiled and have often gone without sleep; I have known hunger and thirst and have often gone without food; I have been cold and naked. Besides everything else, I face daily the pressure of my concern for all the churches."

Lessons Learned

Henri Nouwen, in his book, The Wounded Healer, writes that "a minister is called to recognize the suffer-ings of his time in his own heart and make that recognition the starting point of his service. Whether he tries to enter into a dislocated world, relate to a convulsive generation, or speak to a dying man, his service will not be perceived as authentic unless it comes from a heart wounded by the suffering about which he speaks."

It took years of wrestling with my thorn to come to a place of peace. I must admit that the entire experience has left scars that will never go away. Whenever I reflect on the wounds, they remind me of my vulnerability and my need for total dependence on the Lord. These scars also made me a stronger leader and a more compassionate pastor. I learned to be humble because all it took was one wrong word, one dark thought, one jealous fit to push me into depression. I also learned to forgive, and I began by forgiving myself, my husband, and the woman with which he had the relationship. I also learned the true meaning of unconditional love. Today, I walk in total freedom because I have forgiven myself, my husband and anyone associated with that situation. I also learned that being vulnerable is not a sign of weakness. Vulnerability is the starting point for your emotional and spiritual healing. God gave me a few friends (male and female) with which I could share my emotional pain. They prayed with me, advised me and supported me throughout those critical years.

A friend answered the call of God on her life when she was in her twenties. She joined one of the progressive growing churches in an urban American city and began working with the youth, especially teenage girls. She quickly realized that youth ministry was her passion. Over the ensuing years; I watched her develop a wonderful ministry that positively changed the course of the life of many pre-teens and teens. Unfortunately, she would be struck with a thorn that wounded her and almost destroyed her ministry.

She began experiencing delusionary and other psychotic episodes that pointed to psychological illness. At first, no one understood what the problem was. Like most Christians, her support team of friends and family went through extensive periods of prayers and fasting for her healing. As one psychotic episode followed another, people began to question her mental health and her fitness for ministry. It became apparent that she needed medical professional attention. That was a difficult decision for her because it meant she would have to face her weaknesses, her vulnerabilities, and her thorn.

While she was experiencing this breakdown; she was able to remain focused on her ministry calling. While she was dealing with the stigma of being labeled 'psychotic and delusional,' she was still planning programs, writing workshops and mentoring young girls. We would talk about the confusion she was experiencing and her fear that she would lose her capacity to minister. One thing she never lost was the certainty of her divine calling.

Over fifteen years later, she is living with the thorn of medically managing a mental imbalance; but that thorn has not stopped her from fulfilling her ministry calling in extraordinary ways as a mentor to hundreds of youth, a published author, a college professor and an ordained minister of the gospel.

Leaders are expected to be strong. Leaders are supposed to be without flaw. If they are undergoing a time of trials and emotional pains; they are expected to muster the strength to keep leading and keep the vision moving forward. Followers look to them to always be able to manage their weaknesses.

Jesus taught us that a leader must keep leading even in the midst of pain. The sharp sword at his side reminds me of the thorn in Paul's side and the scars from the thorns my friend and I carry daily. While Jesus hung on the cross, he consoled his mother and provided for her welfare. He administered forgiveness to convicted thieves. He prayed for his persecutors and taught life lessons to the people gathered for his crucifixion. Though he cried out to his Father "My God, my God, why have you forsaken me?" (Matthew 27:46); yet he did not come down off the cross. He was wounded and bruised for our iniquities and yet Jesus kept right on teaching, saving and leading even from the blood-stained cross.

Reflection and Response

Superheroes are fictional comic book characters. We love them because they have supernatural powers, never lose a battle and always capture the bad guys in the end. They are winners! When they show up, we expect success. Have you ever felt like your followers expect you to display flawless leadership at all times? Have you ever come face to face with your shortcomings or do you pretend they don't exist? If so, you have three options:

a) Pretend you are perfect and keep on leading
b) Succumb to your pain and enter a state of leadership paralysis

c) Acknowledge your weakness/pain and pray for grace and strength to stay on the assignment.

Serving while under extreme pressure and pain is very hard. Like Paul, God reminds us that His grace is sufficient for us to endure the scars and the thorns! Thorns are there to teach us to depend on the grace of God for strength, for affirmation, acceptance, and peace. You can follow Paul's example, turn those thorns over to the grace of God and keep on being the leader God called you to be.

What's Your Story?

Journal

Chapter 5

The Invisible Leader

II Samuel 3:7; II Samuel 21: 8,10-14

II Samuel 21: 10a & 14b "Then Rizpah the daughter of Aiah took sackcloth, and spread it on a rock for herself, from the beginning of the harvest until rain fell on them from the heavens; she did not allow the birds of the air to come on the bodies....After that God heeded supplications for the land." (NRSV)

<u>My Story</u>

     *D*uring a regular Sunday morning worship in April 2003 at Empowerment Temple AME Church, two women came to the church and gave a flyer to the usher at the door. The instructions were: "Give this to your pastor to announce during worship. The women of Liberia are meeting to call for an end to the war." After receiving the flyer, I waited for worship to end and then I had a meeting with a few trusted women leaders in my church to discuss the content of the flyer. I wanted to know those who were calling for this mass meeting and whether we could trust them. I was very concerned for our safety. It was war-time. Anyone perceived to be in opposition to the ruling government could vanish without a trace. People were being killed for far lesser reasons than having a meeting. I thought: "the women are depending on me, their pastor, to tell them what to do." We discussed and prayed, and then we all decided to attend the mass meeting.

It had to have been extreme desperation that pushed us to attend the meeting. I did not know any of the orga-nizers. Empowerment Temple was less than two years old, and I was still adjusting to a Liberia at war having been away from home for eleven years. I was also rela-tively unknown and slightly naïve; but, I sensed that the women of my church were desperate to act. The men of Liberia seemed to have run out of ideas, become com-placent or paralyzed by fear. Any action was better than waiting for the next killing spree, the next round of attacks, or the sustained sound of gunfire and missile firing.

We all gathered at the appointed place. Hundreds of women showed up, along with the local and inter-national press. Christian women and Muslim women dressed in white along with many other women packed the hall and spilled over onto the driveway. After a while, a young lady took the microphone and read a position paper stating that the women of Liberia were calling for a cease-fire, peaceful negotiations, and intervention of a peace-keeping force to facilitate the elections of new leadership. The heads of the three warring factions, NPFL, LURD, and MODEL, had received invitations to be present to hear and accept the position paper; however, none of them showed up. Faced with this frustration, the women became angry. How dare these men to ignore them! Whether it was already planned or not; a rallying cry rose up from the women: "We want peace, and we want it NOW!"

The women marched out of that hall and into the streets chanting for peace. They ended their march at an open field along the main highway of the city where everyone sat and prayed. This popular chant captures our state of mind at that time: "Women, Oh Women! Don't just sit there. Do something positive!". The women resolved to stage a nonviolent protest action that would eventually involve thousands of Liberian women and exert enormous pressure on hardened warlords raging a devastating fourteen-year civil war with no end in sight. These events led to the birth of the Women of Liberia Mass Action for Peace (WOLMAP).

WOLMAP was characterized by religious disciplines such as prayer, fasting, all-night vigils, as well as social protest actions such as sit-ins, picketing, marches, rallies, protest speeches, and peace negotiations. This sit-in action lasted for several months, mobilized thousands of women, and spread to three other provinces extending outside Liberia to Ghana, Guinea, and Sierra Leone. On a typical day, women would wake up at 6 am, either climb onto a farm truck, get on a bus or walk miles to an open field where they sat all day. At times groups would be dispatched. With poster and picketing signs in hand, we would stand in a silent protest calling for an end to the war. We picketed Government offices, the United Nations Headquarters in Liberia, the Embassies of the United States of America, Sierra Leone, Cote d'Ivoire, Guinea, Ghana, Nigeria, the European Union, and everywhere we felt necessary. We marched in marketplaces and along major streets of Monrovia. We resolved: no jewelry, no make-up, only a white T-shirt, white head wrap and our traditional wrap skirt (the lappa). I remained involved in the daily activities of WOLMAP until the signing of the Peace Accord and the end of the war in August 2003.

The remarkable thing is that the young lady who read the position paper and became the leader of WOLMAP was an unknown thirty-two-year-old Christian single mother, Leymah Gbowee. Such a leader was a strange phenomenon. For years, male church leadership had been calling for an end to the civil crisis with no success. Both the Liberia Council of Churches and the Interreligious Council of Liberia were engaged in over 13 negotiations and peace conferences. Men headed both of those organizations. At no time did a woman lead those talks and activities.

Without a political or religious title, and in a male-dominated society, Leymah Gbowee deviated from the stereotypical leader. Her background was in social work at the Lutheran outreach center. She was a single mother serving as program coordinator for Women in Peacebuilding Network (WIPNET). Gbowee became the head of the 15-member all-female organizing committee of WOLMAP. It was not by election. It just happened naturally. She inspired us to strategize and mobilize thousands of women into a movement that claimed international attention and is talked about up to the present. With her training in peace-building, she kept the protest action going until the Accra Peace Accord was signed. Later in 2009, she would be awarded the prestigious Nobel Peace Prize. WOLMAP produced an army of invisible leaders because no one appeared to see us, realize our potential nor understand our agenda until it was too late to stop us.

Rizpah's Story

Rizpah (riz'-pa, "coal," "hot stone") was the daughter of Aiah, and one of Saul's concubines. She was the mother of Armoni and Mephibosheth. After the death of Saul, it was rumored that Abner took her as the wife, resulting in a quarrel between him and Saul's son and successor, Ishbosheth. The disagreement led to Abner's defection to David, who was then King of the breakaway Kingdom of Judah. This incident led to the downfall of Ishbosheth and the rise of David as King of a reunited Kingdom of Israel.

During the reign of David, there was a famine for three successive years; so David sought the face of the Lord. The Lord said, 'It is on account of Saul and his blood-stained house; it is because he put the Gibeonites to death'." (2 Sam. 21:1). In the Bible, famine generally is associated with God's disapproval. Prophets usually foretold famine through their visions. In the face of this situation, King David asks God why the nation was experiencing famine, and God would tell him why. In an attempt to solve the national problem, David turns Rizpah's sons along with five other male descendants of King Saul over to be slaughtered by the Gibeonites. With no regard to the anguish this action would cause Rizpah, the sons' mother, Rizpah is a witness to the death of her sons. Their bodies are left on display for all to see without the benefit of a proper burial. Scripture indicates that death by crucifixion and public display of dead bodies carried an extreme negative stigma. "[H]is corpse shall not hang all night on the tree, but you shall surely bury him on the same day (for he who is hanged is accursed of God) so that you do not defile your land which the LORD your God gives you as an inheritance." (Deut. 21:23)

In light of this shame and injustice, Rizpah gets up one morning, dresses in the mourning clothes of sackcloth, and goes to the place of her son's bodies. This grieving mother takes a seat on a rock, and with cloth in hand, she begins to drive away the vultures and wild animals from her dead sons' bodies. This is Rizpah's protest to the manner in which her two sons were killed and their bodies left hanging on a tree.

The story recounts how she sat for at least four months until King David recognized her plight and gave her sons' bones a proper burial; God answered prayer on behalf of the nation. (2 Sam. 21:14). Rizpah, single-handedly, began a non-violent protest against the violence meted on her children.

Lessons Learned

Rizpah had led a hectic and colorful life. It was not a privileged life of honor and prestige. She could not protect herself from Saul's sexual advances, and there was no pathway out of her concubine status. Due to the levirate law of inheritance of wives and concubines, she could not prevent Saul's son Ishobeth from claiming her as his property.

Leymah Gbowee also has a colorful life story. In her memoir, "And Mighty Be Our Powers," she describes her abusive relationship with 'Daniel' the father of four of her children. She talks about finding herself at twenty-six in a place of despair and helplessness. "I was a twenty-six-year-old woman with children who depended on me. I had to take action......My children had suffered so much, and they deserved so much more than they had. I was the only one who could give it to them."(Gbowee 72,73). Rizpah experienced similar feelings of hopelessness and helplessness when King David turned over her two sons to the Gibeonites to be killed. It was just too much to bear.

Both Rizpah and Leymah Gbowee reached a point when they rose out their comatose state and resolved to take action to change their story. Rizpah's move sent the message that she rejected this injustice. She was alone in her protest, but she solicited a reaction from King David that started a chain of events that altered the circumstances of the nation.

First, King Saul is finally laid to rest honorably symbolizing reconciliation between King David and King Saul. Secondly, her innocent sons received an honorable burial. This action removed the stain and disgrace brought on if vultures devour their bodies. Thirdly, her actions moved the heart of God to compassion. God sent the rains, and Israel's drought ended.

The fate of most women is in the hands of men who see them as invisible, inconsequential and insignificant. In

Gbowee's memoir, she talks about how video reports from war stories portray women "fleeing, weeping, kneeling before their children's graves." In the traditional telling of war stories, women are always in the background. Our suffering is just a sidebar to the main tale,"(Gbowee ix)

Georgia Sorenson and Gill R. Hickman argue that great transformation can result from invisible leaders with shared action and possessing a charisma of purpose; therefore, "invisible leadership is a quiet, unobtrusive influence process motivated by strong conviction to a common purpose greater than the self-interest of the group or its members." (Sorenson, Hickman 7).

This narrative illustrates the awesomeness of invisible leadership. No one could have imagined the far-reaching impact of Leymah Gbowee and her band of organizers. No one could believe that Rizpah's seemingly impotent action could bring peace and reconciliation to Israel. Leymah and Rizpah led a movement for healing and reconciliation in their nations.

The Bible recounts stories of women faced with the dilemma of taking action against personal and community threats to their well-being. Contrary to the often-accepted idea of women as the weaker vessel, the weak had to become strong in unusual ways to create a positive paradigm shift in biblical history. Jesus tells the parable of the unjust judge who would not treat a widow fairly. (Luke 18:1-8). Her persistence gained for her the justice she deserved.

How could a relatively unknown, inconsequential woman become a great leader? Rizpah allowed her grief and great love for her sons to propel her to action.

She used what she had, and that was her passionate resistance to her shame. Rizpah was persistent and focused because she was on a mission. I have gotten to know Leymah Gbowee quite well since 2003 during our WOLMAP activities. We would talk about what gave her the courage to do what she did. The seeds of protest began when she realized that her children deserved a better, more just and humane society to live in.

Reflection and Response

Most likely you would not hear of women like Rizpah and Leymah Gbowee. They rise to leadership from a place of obscurity. A spirit of discontent powers them. They do not consider their preparedness but take action out of a need to right a terrible wrong. They are the obscure, invisible leaders who appear suddenly but effect significant change in society.

1. Rizpah understood her powerless condition. A concubine, even of a King, had very little power.
2. Rizpah understood her vulnerability. Embroiled in a love triangle of national proportion, she was a victim of a vicious rumor that Abner was her lover when the Levirite law required that King Saul's son Ishobeth should have taken her as his wife.
3. Rizpah fought for her only valuable asset. Her two sons were all she had because she had lost her social status after the death of King Saul.

Will you open yourself to the possibility of leading change? Will you follow your passion for justice, for peace, for equality until it brings you to a place of authority and power? God is looking for people who will step out of obscurity and be willing to lead. Because Leymah Gbowee stepped out, her advocacy for peace and the empowerment of women is now touching the lives of people on every continent of this world. This invisible leader is now a global voice of peace and leadership, and a champion for girls education and youth empowerment.

What's Your Story?

Journal

_____
_____
_____
_____
_____
_____
_____
_____
_____
_____
_____
_____
_____
_____
_____
_____
_____
_____
_____
_____
_____
_____
_____
_____
_____
_____
_____
_____

Chapter 6

The Negotiating Leader

Texts: I Samuel 25:1-42

I Samuel 25: 32-33 "David said to Abigail, 'Blessed be the Lord, the God of Israel, who sent you to meet me today! Blessed be your good sense, and blessed be you, who have kept me today from bloodguilt and from avenging myself by my own hand!"

<u>My Story</u>

One of the strategies WOLMAP taught us was the art of negotiating in a hostile environment. For over a week the women had been sitting in the open field singing and praying; holding up placards demanding the end to the civil war. President Charles Taylor had not acknowledged our protest action. Because we were strategically sitting where the main highway to the Executive Mansion was; his presidential convoy would take another route to avoid seeing the protesting women. By now, the international press (CNN, BBC, etc.) had taken an interest in us. Their reporters stopped by, took photos and tried to get us to talk. We told them to go and see our leaders. We were not interested in getting our pictures in newspapers or our stories in international magazines. All we wanted was an end to the war. The least our president could do was to stop by and talk to us. President Taylor had already been given a copy of our manifesto for peace. But, all we heard was silence.

We, then, decided to take our protest to the House of Parliament/Capitol Building (where the senators and legislators have their offices). Standing in the pouring rain, with placards lifted high, we waited in silence. After a while, the Speaker of the House of Representatives came out to the women and listened to our request. The word got back to President Taylor that the women had left the field and were standing at the House of Parliament in full view of the international press. As a result of that incident, President Taylor sent WOLMAP an invitation to come to the Executive Mansion to present her case. I am not sure whether he intended for the entire company of hundreds of women to converge at the Executive Mansion or whether the invitation was only for the leader. We decided that all of us would gather there. There is strength in numbers. We thought: "They would have to attack all of us and not target a few."

I admit that I and many others wrestled with the possibility of arrest, imprisonment, or labeled as an enemy of the state. A close male family friend had constantly warned my husband against my participation in WOLMAP. When he heard of the invitation from the President, he stopped by to raise the alarm about the risk of me joining the women to meet the president. "Your good, intelligent wife could be killed," he warned. I could not see how I could stay away from that meeting; though I was afraid. We all prayed, and we discussed, and soon it became clear that this could be an excellent opportunity to advance our cause. After all, this is what we wanted: to be heard!

I remember that sunny day when over a thousand women gathered on the grounds of the Executive Mansion. We all sat on the hot, burning asphalt with no shoes, in white t-shirts, white head ties and lappas (a native skirt) wrapped tight around our waist. Most of us had a pair of trousers under our lappas just in case we had to run. We waited patiently. The word came from the chief of protocol: "The President will see you now, but only the leader and three others. However, he will receive them on the upper floor of the Executive Mansion." I was one of the women selected to represent the group.

This was when the art of negotiation kicked in. If we agreed to a private meeting with the President, we ran the risk of being arrested or even of being accused of taking money (bribe) or even worse of not presenting the case for the women. We were worried about what would happen to the women we left sitting on the grounds. It was a time when no one could be trusted. We were dealing with matters of life and death. We needed to negotiate a compromise.

Here was the situation. The country was at war. The president was leading a nation under siege, embattled, infrastructures destroyed, death and desolation all around with the international community applying pressure on Taylor to leave the seat of power. President Taylor was not in a comfortable place. Maybe, he could use the women to call for a cease-fire from all warring factions, and that would buy him some time to re-strategize? Also, this meeting could send a message to the international community that he was a leader who was not insensitive to the welfare of his people. At the same time, the women needed peace. They needed to farm their land and feed their families. They needed for their children to get back to school. They needed to stop burying their sons and husbands. They needed to reclaim their bodies; no more to be used as sex toys for rampaging fighters. They needed to hear the sound of dancing music and not the sounds of guns and bombs.

Leymah Gbowee relayed the message from the Chief of Protocol to the women. The murmurings of discontent and disappointment started. The women did not like that arrangement at all. We sent our reply to President Taylor. Our plea was that the women needed to see their President and feel that he cared for their plight. They were asking him to lead the way to peace. In their eyes, he sat in the ultimate seat of power. Therefore, could he please come down to the rotunda and speak with their representatives there in full view of the entire mass of women gathered? The language was carefully chosen to emphasize the president's importance and his power. This, of course, appealed to President Taylor's vanity. He wanted to be viewed as the supreme leader and the only one who could take control of the situation. He agreed, and the rotunda was set up with chairs for us along with his gold-painted presidential chair. The pro-temp of the House of Senate was a woman, and she was seated beside the President. She was to serve as a liaison between the president and us.

As the four of us walked up the long flight of stairs, I thought, *"Well, this is it. I will either go to jail today or become a marked woman for future reprisal."* Upon reaching the top of the stairs, we were invited to sit in those beautiful chairs. Leymah Gbowee expressed appreciation for the chairs but insisted we would sit on the floor because right below us the women were sitting on the ground waiting to hear from their president. She said "When the bombs fall, we don't run carrying chairs. We are sharing everything our sisters are going through." (Gbowee,140)

Here we were, no shoes on our feet, seated on the floor while the President sat in his magnificent gold-plated chair. I distinctly remembered Leymah's firm resolve as she read from a prepared statement. The statement repeated our original demands. The women wanted a cease-fire, dialogue among all warring factions and the intervention of an international peace-keeping force and peaceful elections. She ended with this passionate heart-wrenching plea: "we (the women) are now taking this stand, to secure the future of our children. Because we believe, as custodians of society, tomorrow our children will ask us. 'Mama, what was your role during the crisis?'" (Gbowee, 141).

President Taylor listened patiently to her. In responding he spoke about how he was not the only fighting force but that our message had to go out to all of the other leaders of the warring factions. He assured us that he was also tired of the war and would do his part in negotiating an end to the war.

Of course, the war did not end on that day or even the next month. But there were significant gains from that meeting.

1. The Liberian people became more hopeful that there was a chance that the killings and continuous pillage and destruction would end.
2. The international community took note of President Taylor's words and those words would be re-played to keep the pressure on him to "do his part of negotiating an end to the war."
3. The resolve of the women increased. From that experience, delegations would travel to meet with the other warlords and deliver the same message to them. They went to Guinea and Sierra Leone organizing women in those countries to also carry out sit-in protests.

About three months later, the Accra Peace Conference began in Akosombo, Ghana. From there the conference transitioned to Accra, Ghana. Negotiations for a ceasefire went on for more than a month. Finally, the Peace Accord was signed on August 18, 2003. A ceasefire was declared and upheld. Soon after, over 20,000 United Nations peacekeepers landed in Liberia, the war ended, and an interim government was installed. Democratic, peaceful elections were held in 2005 with a woman, Ellen Johnson Sirleaf, elected the President of Liberia.

Abigail's Story

Abigail and David's path would cross because of a crisis. David, now expelled from King Saul's palace, finds himself leading about 600 dissident men. They make their living by attacking the Philistines and raiding their flocks. Besides, David runs a protection racket by sparing the flocks of his countrymen and then demanding payment for doing such.

It is the sheep-shearing season, and David sends a message to Nabal, the husband of Abigail that he requires payment for protecting Nabal's sheep from thieves. Nabal recognizes the extortionist game David is playing and sends an angry response: "Who is this David? Who is this son of Jesse?.... Why should I take my bread and water, and the meat I have slaughtered for my shearers and give it to men coming from who knows where?" (I Sam. 25:11). Nabal's response, in turn, angers David. Pride and anger create a crisis. David commands 400 of his men to arm themselves and prepares to attack Nabal's household with the intent to kill every living being in the compound. David refuses to be ignored and perceived as a weak leader.

One of Nabal's servants hears of the impending attack. With nervous trepidation, he privately informs Abigail, while pleading for her intervention. The scripture describes Nabal as "surly and mean in his dealings." (I Samuel 15:3b). Nabal's attitude explains why the servant hesitated to give this information to him but instead chose to engage Abigail.

Abigail is an exceptional woman: beautiful, quick-thinking and shrewd. Realizing that her husband will stubbornly refuse David's demand, she begins to strate-gize on how to avert the coming disaster. She instructs her servants to gather up food made up of various choice items. This would be her peace offering and a sign to David that she did not agree with her husband's action. She is trying to prevent a confrontation that would be disastrous for both David and Nabal.

While David is on his way to Nabal's house, Abigail meets him on the path: she, her servants and the peace offering. Immediately, Abigail sizes up the situation and appeals to David's hurt pride and ego by begging for forgiveness for her husband's attitude. She is humble, falling at his feet; yet she strongly advises him against allowing Nabal's churlish behavior to goad him to shed innocent blood. The strategy works. David cannot resist the humility, the wisdom and the charm of Abigail.

David is generous in forgiving Nabal and promises not to go forward with the attack. Abigail returns home and attempts to narrate the story to Nabal, but he is in a drunken stupor. At daybreak, Abigail tells him what she has done. Whether angry at her defiance or filled with fear; Nabal suffers a stroke: 'his heart failed him, and he became like a stone.' (I Sam.25:37b) Ten days later, Nabal dies.

Lessons Learned

Scripture describes Abigail, a consummate nego-tiator, as "a woman of good understanding and beau-tiful appearance." (1 Sam. 25:3). Faced with the threat of David and his men raiding her home and killing her family, Abigail skillfully negotiated a peaceful resolution to a potentially dangerous conflict. As a result, she saved many people's lives. She obtained the facts, acted swiftly, and took gifts with her to the negotiation table. In her dialogue with David, she used affirming statements, yet she boldly spoke her mind and openly expressed her desire.

David W. Augsburger states: "Conflict is essential to, ineradicable from, and inevitable in human life; and the source, cause, and process of conflict can be turned from life-destroying to life-building ends." (Augsburger 5). He argues that "Women show a negative orientation toward the use of violent aggression in social, relational or political matters. Violence is increasingly seen as symbolic of male domination and socially pathological. Women show a positive orientation toward negotiation, verbal bargaining, and nonviolent demonstration rather than power, coercion, or violent solutions. Women hold the promise of being more comfortable at the bargaining table and more psychologically inclined toward assertiveness rather than aggression, toward horizontal control rather than vertical control structure." (Augsburger 185)

Miriam Agatha Chinwe Nwoye describes the roles West African women play in peacebuilding and conflict resolution in African traditional societies. Nwoye argues that African women have been not only the center of conflict in society but also in many instances, they have mediated such disputes. The most recent examples they cite are the women of the Mano River region of West Africa.

In her book, Swapping Housewives, Bishop Vashti McKenzie, shares the story of Dr. Lily Sanvee, Medical Director for the St. Joseph Catholic Hospital located in Monrovia, Liberia. Dr. Sanvee talks about attending wounded rebel fighters from different factions who were sharing the same hospital ward. In her words: "It was difficult dealing with them and their leaders at the same time I dealt with my own trauma and problems." (Swapping Housewives 98). Also, Dr. Sanvee had to negotiate protection for the hospital from bomb attacks even as she regularly navigated the threat of conflict and chaos on the wards.

An imminent threat to life produces fertile soil for the springing up of leaders. The war was a constant threat to life in Liberia. The stalemate between David and Nabal was a death threat to Abigail, her family, and her servants. The volatility of opposing wounded rebels sleeping in one room in a hospital ward placed the hospital under threat of siege and destruction. When there is no military strength, money or resources to fight; then creative negotiating comes forward. I believe that God can use us to be negotiating leaders. God is looking for anyone who will see an opportunity for leading during crises.

Reflection and Response

We can never predict when we will find ourselves in the middle of a crisis, some of life-threatening proportion. I find myself replaying that scene from the day we sat looking up at President Taylor seated on his gilded throne. Today, he is serving a 50-year sentence in a jail in the Hague. Because we mastered the art of negotiation, we brokered the peace that Liberia is enjoying today. Negotiation involves giving and taking. It consists of an assessment of strengths and weaknesses. The conversation is all about what each party brings to the negotiating table. The critical thing is that someone has to take the lead to begin the discussion. It is during these times that we look for someone to start the process of bringing calm to a storm, clarity out of chaos and resolution out of a conflict. Have you been in such a situation? Did you play the role of a negotiating leader or did you witness someone else play that role?

How do we overcome fear when God is prompting us to stand up and speak out in a dangerous situation? Take a moment to examine yourself. You may possess the traits of a shrewd, wise negotiator and that may be just what is needed to lead people out of a crisis.

<u>What's Your Story?</u>

Journal

Chapter 7

The Mentoring Leader

Text: I Timothy 4:12-16 and II Timothy 2:1-2

II Timothy 2:1-2 "You then, my child, be strong in the grace that is in Christ Jesus; and what you have heard from me through many witnesses entrust to faithful people who will be able to be teachers as well."

My Story

I vividly recall Sunday, September 30, 2001. The heavy rains were ending in Liberia, and we were greeted with beautiful sunshine that morning. That day would mark the very first worship service of Empowerment Temple African Methodist Episcopal Church. Sixteen proud and excited founding members along with well-wishers, members of sister churches, our personal friends and the general public piled into a small bank lobby (converted into our sanctuary). By 10:30 in the morning, more than one hundred persons had arrived in a room that could seat eighty-five. People were still coming, and there was standing room only. Someone had the foresight to suggest that we set up closed-circuit television in an adjacent office space. We crowded about 30 adults and children in there to view the service.

In the main bank hall, we erected a small wooden dais. Mr. Joseph Boakai, who later served Liberia as vice-president, donated a wooden pulpit to the church. Our church colors are gold, purple and white. A chair, covered with purple velvet fabric, was placed at the center of the dais. That was the pastor's seat. To the left was seating for about ten persons. That would be the choir loft. To the immediate right and left of the pastor's seat were three upholstered chairs for visiting clergy. The backdrop of the dais was a beautiful curtain made of purple and gold drapery with a cross at the center. I was the founding pastor and the only minister on staff. We did not have a licentiate, a deacon, a local deacon/elder, a licensed evangelist nor an elder. I was it!!

At that first worship service, the sixteen members became the choir when it was time for selections; ushers at the door, alternatively carrying out every other function. It was almost comical to watch them go up to the choir loft; then move down to usher; a few of the women navigating their way to serve as stewardesses.

I mastered the art of multi-tasking. I was the worship leader, and I gave the invocation, I read the scripture, I preached the sermon, I presented the invitation to Christian discipleship, I received and blessed the offering, conducted the communion service and pronounced the benediction. I faced my small congregation every Sunday morning poised to execute my duties with diligence and precision.

I am grateful to my now-deceased uncle, Reverend George Timothy Wilson, Sr. At that time, he was a retired Presiding Elder. Every first Sunday he came and assisted me with the Communion Service. One day he gave me this advice: "You know the lay people can participate in the order of worship. Get your stewards to help you conduct worship." Later, he would encourage me with these words: "God will raise up preachers in this church."

I quickly realized that I needed help, when, to my great satisfaction, the membership grew to one hundred persons by the beginning of 2002. The men's department was the first to get organized; quickly followed by the women and other auxiliaries. From the onset, we already had at our Boards of Trustee and Steward in place. The choir director was appointed. Soon, we added more chairs on the dais for singers. We organized the Sunday School to accommodate the increase in the number of children. However, I remained the lone clergy in the pulpit.

In late 2002, a young, energetic itinerant deacon, Reverend Tarkolo Miller, was assigned to serve at Empowerment Temple. He was an ordained itinerant deacon, equipped with strong administrative and preaching skills. This was a blessing. The problem was that Reverend Miller was a product of another AME Church and had recently been removed from pastoring there. His removal by the bishop was not well-received. This resulted in protests and congregational resistance.

When Reverend Miller came to Empowerment Temple, he was a superannuated minister. Superannuated pastors are those who ask for and are granted time off from active ministry in an AME church. The move to Empowerment worked out well, and it afforded him a path out of super-annuation. He served well; but, I knew that Empowerment had to birth her sons and daughters that I could teach and guide into ordination. Later, Reverend Miller would move on from Empowerment Temple and accept a different pastoral assignment.

Subsequently, two young men at Empowerment Temple came forth and expressed their desire to preach the gospel. I was excited. I had no experience in these matters, and I made the mistake of pre-maturely affirming their calling. Later, I discovered that they were driven by pulpit power more than by the desire go through the training process required on the journey to ordination in the AME Church. These two guys did not last long, and they left to join other denominations.

During that period, a lady joined the church, and it became evident that she was spiritually gifted. She came out from one of the charismatic Pentecostal churches. This woman was a very committed intercessor. I appointed her to head the Intercessory Prayer Ministry. Again, I failed to recognize her character flaws which significantly compromised her integrity and almost brought disrepute to Empowerment Temple. Over time, I began to receive complaints. She was requesting financial payment in exchange for time spent in prayer sessions with members and non-members. This was extortion and a money-making game. I had to decide to remove her from the clerical staff and suspend her membership at the church. That was another blow in my quest to raise ministers at Empowerment Temple.

Then came Emmanuel Armah Seh. Years later, he explained to me how he felt the undeniable call of God to ordained ministry; but he resisted for several reasons. He thought he was too poor and with little to offer. He was a high school graduate and had no financial means of entering the university. He was a petty trader toiling under the hot African sun pushing his wheelbarrow of goods for sale. He was from rural southwest Liberia; not a city boy. He said that he felt intimidated by me because I was smart, well-educated and attractive. How would I even receive him and would he measure up to my standards? He was shy and had very low self-esteem. He would not come forward to acknowledge that call until Reverend Miller pushed and prodded him to make a move.

After a long period of soul-searching, he found the courage to inform me of his desire to enter the ministry. He served Empowerment Temple consistently and faithfully for fourteen years. His journey was not without setbacks and challenges. Yet, he was able to complete seminary as well as earn a graduate degree in Education. His last assignment was the Administrative Minister at Empowerment Temple. He was to me as Elisha was to Elijah. He is now serving his first assignment as a pastor of one of our local churches. Like Paul released young Timothy to serve as a pastor, so Reverend Emmanuel Seh is released from Empowerment Temple.

Right after ordination, I plunged into pastoring and establishing a church. It was difficult to train and mentor church leadership while I was also going through a time of training and mentorship as a first-time pastor. In the shortest time, I decided that the best route would be through workshops and seminars. My classroom teaching approach came from a place of familiarity. I was a teacher; so, I taught. While others mentored by show and tell, try and correct, or command and perform; I taught them the principles I learned from books.

In retrospect, Reverend Seh tells me that he learned more from watching me; but, at that time, I was not sure that I was giving the best performance. At that time, I firmly believed that the way to do it was written some-where in a book, on the internet, or at a training seminar.

I am happy to report that Reverend Emmanuel Seh was joined over the years by fourteen other ministers to serve at Empowerment Temple. I realize that those who are now elders have become the primary go-to teachers for the licentiates and lay leadership. There is a phrase in the world of human resource development: "trainers of trainers." These elders are now the mentoring leaders of licentiates and lay leaders. They have become trainers of trainers and leaders of leaders.

The Story of Paul & Timothy

The apostle Paul is considered the most influential bib-lical figure in the history of Christianity (aside from Jesus Christ). As an apostle, he planted more churches, wrote more biblical text, offered more teachings on Christian prin-ciples, and mentored more believers than any of the eleven disciples. However, Paul was once called Saul, and he was once the most forceful advocate for the extermination of followers of Jesus Christ. He was a Roman citizen by birth, grew up in Tarsus and educated in both the Greek-Roman cultures. Saul also trained as a tentmaker. He also had a thorough knowledge of Judaism and the Jewish scriptures.

However, Paul (formerly Saul), perceived his life mission was to prevent the spread of Christianity by violently destroying it. He was actively involved in capturing followers of Jesus Christ and turning them over to the authorities in Jerusalem for persecution. Paul was very effective at it, and his name was feared far and wide among the new believers.

Acts chapter 9 records the story of Paul's conversion through a miraculous encounter with Jesus Christ while he (Paul) was on the Damascus road on a mission to arrest believers. The encounter was so definitive that Paul entered into the life of a believer with the same level of zeal and passion with which he had tried to destroy the church.

An important note is that he was an outsider, a novice to the ministry. (Acts 9: 20-26). Paul traveled to Jerusalem to preach. This was met with great suspicion. The disciples would not immediately affirm his divine calling. There were many others led by the eleven disciples of Jesus who did not trust him. Over time, proof of Paul's calling would be affirmed through conversions of Gentiles, signs, and miracles. Peter and the apostles finally embraced him.

Young Timothy met Paul something during Paul's early years in ministry. Paul was on an evangelism mission in Timothy's hometown Lystra located in South East Asia Minor. It was then that Timothy became converted. A few years later the apostle Paul came through Lystra for a second trip, and that is when Timothy joined him as a traveling missionary. He remained with Paul throughout his entire ministry.

Like Paul, Timothy would come from a mixed background. Timothy's mother was a Jewish Christian, and his father was a Gentile. To avoid the backlash from Jewish Christians who insisted that all new converts should be circumcised; Paul had Timothy circumcised. (Acts 16: 1-3). The relationship between Paul and Timothy was a mentoring one. What is noteworthy is that Paul was also going through a time of spiritual self-discovery and spiritual self-affirmation of his calling and ministry while mentoring Timothy and Titus, his assistants.

"to Timothy, my true son in the faith.." I Timothy 1:2
"To Titus, my true son in our common faith.." Titus 1:4

Timothy was stationed in Ephesus when Paul sent him the pastoral letters. These letters not only contained Paul's instructions on spiritual church matters but also included mentoring tips and admonitions specifically to help Timothy become a better leader to the people.

Paul examined the reputation of Timothy and accepted Timothy to work with him in ministry. He taught him, empowered him, equipped him and trusted him with major leadership tasks.

Lessons Learned

Paul was an emerging leader and at the same time a mentoring leader. Peter, the titular head of the movement had spent three years under the guidance and teaching of Jesus Christ. He had first-hand experience. Peter understood the mission and was a witness to the power of the gospel. He focused on spreading that gospel, winning souls and advancing the cause of Jesus Christ.

Paul's conversion came through spiritual intervention. He did not have the benefit of being taught first hand by Jesus. His conversion was a 360-degree turn in the opposite direction of his life. His focus was different. Paul constantly reminds us that he was sent primarily to convert the Gentiles. (Acts 22:21, Galatians 1;15-16, Galatians 2:9).

In Romans 15: 20-21, Paul writes "and thus I aspired to preach the gospel, not where Christ was already named, so that I would not build on another man's foundation; but as it is written, 'They who had no news of him shall see, and they who have not heard shall understand."

Like Paul, I was a newcomer; actually, a latecomer to the ministry. I, like Paul, believed that I was already on my set path fulfilling my life's purpose as a teacher. I was called into ministry when I least expected. Like Paul, I began preaching in unchartered waters. In Liberia, I did not have the mentorship and support that I had enjoyed at Payne Memorial AME Church in Baltimore. I was accused of forming a break-away church and of stealing members from one of the prominent AME churches in the city. I was received with suspicion. That is why it became critical for God to send me persons who I could mentor into leadership and who would be committed to the ministry of Empowerment Temple. Though Paul was spreading the gospel; Paul was also training and mentoring 'sons and daughters in the ministry who would continue the work long after his death. This was a key secret to his success. In addition to Timothy, there was Titus, Barnabas, Phoebe, Silas and so many more.

I remember the day that Reverend Emmanuel Seh received his first pastoral appointment. Not only would he be leaving Empowerment Temple; but, the Bishop transferred him into a different annual conference from Empowerment Temple. I had less than a day to deal with this reality. We were a great team. He was my right-hand, and he was leaving. The Lord quickly revealed to me that this was not a setback, but I should see this as the litmus test of my leadership. *Did I do a good job of mentoring Reverend Seh?*

Two months into his new assignment, Reverend Seh posted this message on social media: "God first, but you are the reason for the educated, trained, humble and professional man in me. You never denied me your good, good knowledge. You insured that I got the best training from you and I am thankful." I am not only very proud of this young man, but I see his success as a real test of my leadership ability. Leaders produce great leaders. That is the true meaning of legacy.

Reflection and Response

You may be called to begin your ministry or fulfill a vision in unchartered territory and under unknown circumstances. If this is your situation, I want to encourage you to trust God to reveal to you how to teach and mentor others. God will map out a strategy that works best for you and your people.

Let me share with you what has worked for me

1. identify potential leaders either through their self-discovery or my insightful discovery
2. invest time deliberately and routinely in training while exposing them to seminars/workshops to develop their gifts and talents
3. delegate responsibilities to them where they are the left alone to lead
4. give them healthy, thoughtful, sincere feedback
5. encourage them to mentor others into leaders
6. don't give up if the one you mentor falls short of your expectations. Keep looking for others to mentor.

As you accept the challenge of leadership, you also have to take responsibility for mentorship. In the closing verses of I Timothy, Paul says:

"Timothy, guard what has been entrusted to your care. Turn away from godless chatter and opposing ideas of what is falsely called knowledge, which some have professed and in so doing have wandered from the faith." (I Timothy 6:20-21a). By this, Paul was ensuring that his leadership legacy would not die.

What's Your Story?

Journal

_____
_____
_____
_____
_____
_____
_____
_____
_____
_____
_____
_____
_____
_____
_____
_____
_____
_____
_____
_____
_____
_____
_____
_____
_____
_____
_____

Chapter 8

The Risk-Taking Leader

The Book of Nehemiah

Nehemiah 2:17 "You see the trouble we are in: Jerusalem lies in ruins, and its gates have been burned with fire. Come, let us rebuild the wall of Jerusalem, and we will no longer be in disgrace."

<u>My Story</u>

On September 11, 2001, amid shocking news of terrorist attacks on the towers of the World Trade Center in New York City, nine persons met me in Monrovia, Liberia where I unfolded the vision to establish an AME Church. Seven more would join us at the subsequent meetings. Sixteen persons became the founding members. The most urgent concern was finding a place of worship. It appeared that we would have to rent a hall. One

YOU CAN LEAD!

of the founding members was a shareholder in a defunct bank, and the bank building was now empty. We were granted the use of the banking floor and three offices. The banking floor was converted to be used for the worship hall. The pastor had the use of one office. The other two offices were for Sunday school and administration.

The bank lobby could accommodate about 75 persons seated. We soon outgrew the tiny bank lobby and asked permission to put a roof on a large garage space to convert it into our sanctuary. This was the beginning of the first infrastructure development of Empowerment Temple. A church, less than one-year-old, found herself starting a building project. In the previous chapter, I shared the difficulty of leading under these circumstances. My challenge was balancing the training of church leadership while I was also going through a time of preparation and mentorship as a first-time pastor. Think about that. Now add on a church building project!

We were compelled to build because we had run out of space. My husband, Jim, was serving as the pro-tempore of the Trustee Board and together we led our church into a season of giving. Within three months the roof was on, and the hall was made ready for worship. The members practically did the work with their bare hands. Women painted the walls and men laid the concrete blocks and did the carpentry work. It was a wonderful time of sharing and working together. Because there were no available jobs, most of our members volunteered to be unskilled laborers. Fortunately, we had three members- a bricklayer, a contractor, and a carpenter, who formed the construction leadership. We spent so much time at the church that we took our daily meal together.

This first building project solidified the membership. Everyone felt like family. We had our first experience of what it means for believers to trust God and unite behind a shared vision. We planned for growth so the converted garage could accommodate three hundred persons. However, there was only one bathroom and two small offices. Nevertheless, we were satisfied and very proud of our achievement. The ministry was growing and thriving. This first venture was not overly costly, and everyone pitched in to make it happen. In April of 2003, we proudly welcomed our Bishop and many guests to dedicate our new worship space.

By 2005, the owners of the bank building decided that they wanted to renovate and lease the building. The civil war was over. Liberia had elected a president, and the country was on the way to peace and stability. The economic wheels began to turn, and businesses started re-opening. We could no longer remain in a prime down-town property without paying a considerable amount of rent. We were given the notice to leave in twelve months. It was my task to seek the will of God for a suitable place for us to move. The consensus was that we should buy or build a permanent worship edifice. After consultations with our episcopal leader, Bishop Richard Franklin Norris, Sr., with the consent of the Liberia Annual Conference, a piece of property was turned over to us to serve as our permanent home. The property was in a terrible condition. The roof was off, the walls were broken down, and the floors damaged. Remaining walls had extensive cracks. The foundation was sinking. There were no windows, doors nor bathroom fixtures. Tall grass and weeds overran the entire property. The civil war had taken its toll on that building! On the positive side, the building was very spacious, at an ideal location and held great potential for a church with a vision like Empowerment Temple.

On our fourth church anniversary (2005) we launched Operation Roof Empowerment Temple. This Operation included a renovation, rebuilding, and roofing project estimated at $100,000.00 (United States Dollars). The membership was holding at about two hundred persons. The average monthly income was $150.00 (United States Dollars) a month. Throughout two years, the members diligently paid into a capital fund (Operation Roof Empowerment) and raised over 30,000.00 dollars.

Meanwhile, the church obtained a bank loan for the remaining amount. We rebuilt the walls, fixed the bathrooms, put up the steel trusses and the roof. We held our first worship service in our new home on New Year's Eve 2007. On the first Sunday in 2008, we proudly dedicated our roof and honored all the people who contributed to this project. This project was a significant milestone, moving from a garage space to a three-story building. I was very optimistic about our success, in part to naiveté, due to how well things worked out with the first building project back in 2002. But we also experienced some negative fallout.

The members were very supportive at the onset of Operation Roof Empowerment. However, like those cracks in the physical structure so cracks developed in the ministry of Empowerment Temple. To name the most important ones:

- Some members thought that the project was too big for such a small congregation.
- Others felt that the building project removed the focus from evangelistic spiritual outreach to more fund-raising.
- Others got tired of the long giving process needed to raise the desired amount.
- Others did not fully not fully appreciate the cost of the project and felt that the project cost was inflated.

Looking back over the past seventeen years; I can say that 2005-2007 were my most difficult years as a pastor. Empowerment lost members during that time. The burden of this big vision, the sacrificial giving required and the change in location created discouragement in some members. They simply left to join other churches.

Unfortunately, the completion of the project suffered a six-month delay until we could bring in a roofer from Nigeria. We discovered that our builders had misled us. They were unable to put up the roofing sheets. The design of the sanctuary required the roof to be installed at a height of 100 feet. We made inquiries all over Liberia for another builder to install the roof. No one could be found. We were paying a bank loan, and at the same time the steel trusses were already built and had been laying on the floor for months. Time was running out. We had a

"Notice to Vacate" in our possession, and we needed to leave our downtown site.

I remember one night, I lay on the bedroom floor sobbing and pleading with God to remove the obstacles and move the project forward. After a while, my husband, Jim, asked me: "Why are you crying so bitterly?". I kept sobbing out that I was tired and the people are getting tired, and the money is not coming on time, and there was no one to put on the roof. I wanted to give up. I will never forget Jim's response: "Isn't that building called the house of the Lord? That's not your house so stop crying. The Lord will build his house." And the Lord sure did!

Nehemiah's Story

We encounter Nehemiah living in exile in Persia. He is serving as the personal aid to King Artaxerxes. During a typical day, Nehemiah brings a cup of wine to the king and the king realizes that Nehemiah is looking sad and downhearted. The king inquires as to the cause of this demeanor. Nehemiah is afraid to explain and then musters the courage to tell King Artaxerxes that terrible news is coming out of Jerusalem. The wall of the city is broken down. The people are downhearted. Hence, Nehemiah is distraught and wants to go to Jerusalem and help in the rebuilding of the city wall.

Amazingly, the king grants him a leave of absence, signs a personal letter to provide for safe passage across checkpoints and authorizes the gift of building materials. Nehemiah, with a determined mind, travels to Jerusalem and begins the rebuilding project. His first act is to conduct a quiet, but thorough assessment of the extent of the damages. He faces the reality of the enormity of the task and then gathers the people to launch the project. Here are his words to them: "You see the trouble we are in: Jerusalem lies in ruins, and its gates burned with fire. Come, let us rebuild the wall of Jerusalem, and we will no longer be in disgrace." (Neh.2:17).

Opposition arises. Two influential Samaritan leaders, Tobias and Sanballat, argue against Nehemiah's rebuilding project. They did not want Nehemiah to succeed because they knew that would mean the rebirth of Jerusalem to prominence. Nehemiah has to navigate through the negative push-back from other Jews who sided with Tobias and Sanballat. Nehemiah had to inspire the people to trust him.

Throughout the Book of Nehemiah, he would experience times of discouragement and rejection. In chapter 5 of the book of Nehemiah, the people would refuse to work because of the financial strain they were experiencing. "Now the men and their wives raised a great outcry against their Jewish brothers. Some were saying 'we and our sons and daughters are numerous; in order for us to eat and stay alive, we must have grain.' Others were saying 'We have had to borrow money to pay the king's tax on our fields and vineyards'. (Neh.5:1-4). Nehemiah could not ignore those complaints and took the time to devise means to settle them. Nehemiah would continually seek divine wisdom to handle these myriad challenges. The good news is that he remained focused, dealt with every crisis and led the people to successful completion of the rebuilding of the wall of Jerusalem.

Lessons Learned

Establishing a new church and embarking on an extensive capital development campaign within a five-years period is not something I would recommend to a first-time pastor. You are trying to grow the church on four significant levels at the same time: vision casting, membership expansion, spiritual growth, and infrastructure expansion. The people have to hear the vision, understand the vision and then own the vision as theirs. Empowerment Temple was birthed during the civil war when every facet of Liberia was inundated by destruction and decay. Pipe born water was scarce, and electricity came through privately-owned expensive generators. This ministry was centered around the theme of hope and empowerment for the individual. New members had in mind that they had found a place that would cater to them. This was post-war Liberia. Members needed education, jobs, skills training, rent money, and even food money. Here I was asking church members to make personal sacrifices at a time when they had minimal resources.

Opposition to our second building project was not as direct and overt as in the case of Tobias and Sanballat. The opposition was subtle. Members began to stop coming to church regularly. Some started rumblings and murmurings that the church should be helping people and not asking people for money. Initially, I was oblivious to this state of affairs. I am thankful for the loyal board members who were very committed to the project. I now am aware that they deliberately shielded me from the criticisms. Besides, I had my struggle with the fear of failure.

My response was to exude stoic courage and optimism whenever I faced the membership. Privately, I had many moments of doubt and fear.

As I read through Nehemiah's story, it's evident that he was a leader who kept his focus on the finish line. Every obstacle or resistance was an opportunity to rethink, retool and revise the strategy. A valuable lesson I have learned is that I don't have to do it all right now. Success is a journey, and sometimes the timelines have to be adjusted to accommodate personal ability and available resources. Some projects may require marathon leadership rather than sprint leadership. The idea is to get to the finished line. I learned that flexibility is critical. A plan provides a framework for the vision to develop and take shape. There must be room for adjustment to avoid frustration. Another valuable lesson is that leaders should avoid being motivated by competition. Do not spend your time comparing your progress with another ministry/institution down the street. Each one is unique with its distinctive strategic plan. Remain faithful to your plan until you reach the finished line.

Reflection and Response

Leaders carry the future in their hearts and minds, and the future is always bigger than the present resources can support. When that leader speaks that vision; the followers may not immediately see it or may become paralyzed when faced with the reality of the high cost involved; hence the people may abandon the vision. Jesus' disciples had their moment of doubt, and Peter asked the question of Jesus: "We have left everything to follow you. What then will there be for us?" (Matthew 19: 27). Think about the following.

1) Are you or have you been tempted to reject a big vision because you cannot see where the resources are coming from?
2) Do you find yourself taking on too many critical ventures/campaigns at the same time?
3) Are you paying attention to the response of your people as you embark on a big project?
4) What steps can you take to keep a balance between your people's needs and the project's needs?

The response of Jesus to Peter's question tells us that Jesus was sensitive to their need for remunerations. He said "I tell you the truth, at the renewal of all things....... you who have followed me will also sit on twelve thrones, judging the twelve tribes of Israel, And everyone who has left houses or brothers or sisters or father or mother or children or fields for my sake will receive a hundred times as much and will inherit eternal life." (Matt. 19:28-29)

What's Your Story?

Journal

Chapter 9

The Teachable Leader

Acts 18: 24-28; I Corinthians 3: 5-9; Titus 3:13

I Cor. 3: 6: "I planted the seed. Apollos watered it, but God made it grow."

<u>My Story</u>

*M*y father constantly bragged about my intelligence. As far back as I can remember, I recall my father pointing to me and telling total strangers: "You know, my daughter is brilliant." Of course, I loved the compliments and would smile and beam whenever he said those words. He had good reason to say that because I skipped the 2nd and the 4th grades. When at the end of the school year, your final average is 100% in every subject and teachers can tell that you are not academically challenged; you are 'double promoted.' This was the way

it was in Liberia during the 1960s. I subsequently graduated high school at age 16, completed university at age
20; was married at age 22 and had obtained my graduate
degree at age 24 with my first child on the way.

The plan was I would be the first medical doctor in the
York family. This was the only profession worthy of such
intelligence. But, though I had the grades, I did not have the
heart. After two years of pre-med courses, I went on to graduate with a Bachelors in Zoology, minor in Chemistry and
a Master of Science in Biology (emphasis Microbiology). I
became a science teacher, loving every minute of it.

At the time of God's call to ministry in 1995, I wondered about all those years as a science teacher. I could
not understand why God would have allowed me to spend
precious time pursuing a career as an educator; only to
place me on a career path that would require me to go
back to school. I thought to myself: *"Theology is as far
from Biology as the east from the west. This is science
meeting spirit, fact meeting faith, and tested information
meeting divine revelation. How would that work?"*.

In the Baltimore Annual Conference, the rule of the
AME Church was that only persons with a Masters of
Divinity are eligible for full ordination. Here I was, a refugee, well-educated and finding myself faced with the
prospect of going back to school for a second graduate
degree. I must admit this was tough to accept; but, I faced
up to the task and God granted me success. I graduated
from Wesley Theological Seminary in 2001 just on track
to be ordained an itinerant elder that same year.

I returned to Liberia in that same year, education-
ally well positioned. In that region, I was the only AME

with a graduate degree in theology. I immediately began teaching at the John R. Bryant Theological Seminary (BTS) and the Liberia Baptist Theological Seminary. In a few years, I rose to the position of Dean of the Seminary at BTS. Empowerment Temple was in her baby years (2001-2005) and experiencing a significant growth trend.

One thing I did observe was that our growth was more horizontal than vertical. The number of ministries was increasing; but, the individual lives were not growing deeper into the soil of the spirit. I had the knowledge, the education, and passion; but, I perceived that the members were not rooted enough in the scripture and their relationship with Christ. I began to notice a quick turn-over of members. A person would join today, and we would not see them until four Sundays later.

I started new programs; hoping that would keep the people busy. Most of the programs would thrive for a little while then die out. My mother used to warn me that I would wear my members out. I thought I was stimulating them to grow. To be fair, Liberia was coming out of major civil conflict, and people migration was common. Church members were flooding the American and European embassies seeking visas with the intent of relocating to a better life. Also, the trauma and ravages of war and erosion of hope made people very skeptical of anyone in authority and that included pastors.

In 2005, after some degree of painful self-examination; I faced the truth that I needed to learn more about this phenomenon called "pastoring." I needed to be schooled though I already possessed a theological degree. I began attending conferences and workshops sponsored by other church leaders. Some of them were not seminary trained, but they understood some fundamental dynamics of ministry that I had not learned in seminary. I wanted to lead my people better; therefore, I became an eager student.

By 2007, I thought we had finally achieved a good balance: strong teaching, anointed preaching and great administration. We were about to move into a new building which would be large enough to accommodate the big vision God had given us. Plans were on the way to open an elementary school. It was an exciting time. I was settling into my comfort zone. The church was stabilizing, healthy (or so I thought).

In early 2008, the opportunity to enroll in the Beeson Scholars Program came my way. I could attend Asbury Theological Seminary and obtain a Doctor of Ministry degree with all expenses paid. I immediately jumped at the opportunity. I was accepted, began studies in 2008, and graduated in 2012 with honors.

During those four years (2008-2012), I was out two times a year up to seven weeks each time. Every time I would leave, the members would slack off, the work would slow down, the giving would decrease. At times, confusion would break out. I remember that it was during one of my absences that the entire male chorus went on strike and since then, has not re-organized. Though there were other clergy at the church, the people's attention was centered on me. Each time I returned, I had to re-energize the people and reach out to those who had 'sat out' and coax them to return to church. I felt like I was babysitting rather than leading. It was frustrating to have to re-do what had already been done!

Leading while pursuing academic studies is difficult; but informative. I remember sitting in my leadership cohort at Asbury Theological Seminary and asking the question "When can a pastor count on the people to just show up and serve even when the pastor is not present?" My professor asked me to share the history of Empowerment. I told him the church was eight years old and I was the founder. He said you don't start to count on anybody until the church is at least ten years old. He suggested that I may be contributing to the problem because I had taught my people about leadership; but, I had not let them lead. I was teaching well, but I was not leading well.

This was a wake-up call for me. I held a church-wide leadership retreat around the theme "Who Are We?". I re-structured the clerical staff. I appointed Reverend Emmanuel Seh as the Administrative Minister to coordinate all church organizations' work. I empowered the laity to lead their organizations and removed clergy from oversight duties transferring that responsibility on to members of the Boards of Stewards and Trustees. I stopped being the lead bible study teacher and allowed other clergy persons to plan and teach bible studies.

Since completing the Doctor of Ministry, I have been on the campaign trail for episcopal leadership in the AME Church. During the years 2012-2016, I had to travel away from the church even more. The church has successfully transitioned to a level of maturity that I can plant, others can water, and God will faithfully give the increase. As recently as 2018, the records from a 2-month vacation revealed that in my absence, the giving increased by 15% when it used to decrease by 50% during my absence. Now, the laity is fully prepared and ready to 'grow their church.' Organizations do their work plan, organize their events and take the initiative with new and creative ideas. Now, all I do is review proposals, give feedback and approve. I started taking Monday's off for what I call 'personal fulfillment time' (PFT). I do not go to the church office. During PFT, I choose to work on writing books, paint, lay in the bed, go shopping or whatever fulfills me at that time.

Apollos Story

The apostle Paul travels to Corinth and meets a Jew named Aquila. Aquila and his wife Priscilla have recently been expelled from Italy by the Caesar Claudius who ordered all Jews to leave Rome. Paul, Silas, Timothy, and others are all in Corinth preaching the gospel. They remained there for over a year. Paul, Aquila, and Priscilla decided to sail to Ephesus to carry on the ministry journey.

Paul subsequently leaves the husband and wife team in Ephesus. Most likely, Paul is confident that they are well-grounded and equipped to carry on the work. Meanwhile, Apollos, a Jew, originally from Alexandra, comes to Ephesus. The text describes Apollos as "a learned man, with a thorough knowledge of the scriptures. He had been instructed in the way of the Lord, and he spoke with great fervor and taught about Jesus accurately, though he knew only the baptism of John. He began to speak boldly in the synagogue. When Priscilla and Aquila heard him, they invited him to their home and explained to him the way of God more adequately." (Acts 18:24-26)

Apollos is brilliant but inadequate. He is a strong leader, but he has some deficiencies. Apollos accepts the instructions from the husband/wife team. He is willing to be taught in order to improve himself. Apollos goes on to Achaia where he is of great help to the believers because now he can more vigorously and accurately convince others to follow the teachings of Jesus.

However, all is not well in Corinth. A few years later, Paul hears about divisions and quarrels over who the people should follow. He is disappointed with the disunity in the church. He describes the Corinthian Christians as behaving like babies feeding on milk because of their spiritual immaturity. Paul accuses them of acting worldly, like mere men because they quarrel among themselves as to who to follow. "some say 'I follow Paul and another 'I follow Apollos." (I Cor. 3:4)

Paul admonishes them that both he and Apollos are just servants of the Lord assigned to do specific tasks. Paul puts it like this: "I planted the seed. Apollos watered it, but God made it grow." (I Cor. 3: 6). Paul wants them to understand that Apollos because he was willing to be taught, was fit for the work of leading their community. The good news is that reconciliation occurred, the people got over their divisions, and the ministry progressed under Apollos.

Lessons Learned

We need the planters. Paul planted, I planted.

We need the waterers. Apollos watered, clergy and other church leadership watered.

We need growth. God grows the seed.

95

Planting is one time, watering is a daily task.

God used this period of crisis when I was away from the church to expose the immaturity that led to disunity and inconsistency in the church.

1) I learned that leading is not a "one person show." I prayed for the release from the notion that, since I established Empowerment Temple, she was my baby, my full responsibility and no one could take care of her as well as I could.

2) I learned that the break down came when there were no waterers prepared and empowered to water the seed. It has to be more than telling people how it should be. The next step is letting people do what should be done and holding them accountable.

3) I had to change some leaders in the middle of their term. I had to cancel some new programs because there was no 'water' for them. I had to adjust the roles people play.

All of this is part of the learning process. I, the planter, had to trust the Aquilas', Priscillas' and Apollos', to do the work when I could not be there.

Every challenge can be a teachable moment. Leadership gaps are created from a lack of understanding that God uses each of us for a specific task. That's why leaders should never stop learning. A leader must continuously be a student because we need effective planters, but the planter must ensure that the waterers are also learning. Paul had to leave; but, Aquila and Priscilla taught

Apollos and prepared him to be an effective waterer. Apollos was open to corrections, eagerly embracing new information. Apollos went on to do great ministry. He made sure that Paul's seed did not go un-watered.

The story does not end there. Later, Paul instructs his protégée, Titus, to make sure to help Apollos with the work and see to it that he has everything he needs. (Titus 3:13). Help comes to the one who makes the sacrifice and who is willing to remain teachable. The needs of the ministry are supplied, and continuity is ensured. Learning and leading can be the right formula for continuous ministry growth.

<u>Reflection and Response</u>

Have you observed that leaders who succeed are always in a student mode? These leaders are always trying to satisfy their desire for more information, more training, and more wisdom. If you want to attain your goals successfully, you must make the sacrifice to get the education, enroll in the training classes and keep going after the latest information in your chosen career. For many leaders, the time and effort spent in pursuing a degree can take away from time needed at the church or office. Are you feeling guilty for spending so much time away from your congregation? I know of pastors who use that as an excuse for not obtaining the necessary theological education. Be warned: A leader who stops learning is a failed leader.

If you are faced with this dilemma, consider your answers to these questions:

1. Do you believe that obtaining a graduate degree in your chosen field is an essential asset for excellence in leadership?
2. Do you attend leadership training and seminars in your chosen field at least three times a year?
3. Do you require your staff to attend training and workshops in their chosen field on a regular basis?
4. Do you have a plan to evaluate and assess your team and offer suggestions for improvement?
5. Do you read current books on your chosen field and apply innovative ideas in your church/institution?
6. Do you teach your followers to accept to be prepared and led by members of your staff?
7. Do you deliberately step away from leadership and allow others who have been trained to lead?
8. Are you willing to accept that effective growth of a ministry is facilitated through teamwork?

You can still learn and lead if you invest in empowering others to learn and lead.

<u>What's Your Story?</u>

Journal

Chapter 10

The Waiting Leader

The Book of I Samuel & II Samuel chapters 1-5

Psalm 27:14 "Wait for the Lord; be strong and take heart and wait for the Lord."(NIV)

<u>My Story</u>

*L*et me go back and outline the trajectory of my journey as a leader who waits. After realizing that I was not destined to pursue a career in medicine, I re-visited my childhood desire to be a teacher. My mother was a teacher. When a child, she would take me to her classes. I would sit in the back with my books and other school material and say to myself: *"I want to be just like her and do just what she is doing."* I would go on to teach high school biology and chemistry for fourteen years and university biology courses for five years. Much later in life,

I did a gift assessment which confirmed that my strongest gift is teaching.

Every four years, there is a connectional meeting of the Women Missionary Society of the African Methodist Episcopal Church. In 1975, I was chosen to be among three young adults to be the first from the 14th Episcopal District to travel as delegates to the Women's Quadrennial Convention held in Washington, DC- USA. I am grateful to the late Bishop Frank Madison Reid, Jr. who gave us that opportunity. While in my twenty's, I remember serving as a junior stewardess at Eliza Turner AME Church assisting the older women to prepare the Lord's Supper every first Sunday. During those years, I did not know one day that I would have to assume the mantle of a pastor with the formidable task of leading God's people.

These events happened before the start of the Liberian civil war in 1990. While Liberia was engulfed in civil conflict, I was in America worshipping at Payne Memorial AME Church. I had developed an insatiable need for spiritual fulfillment. I thirsted for the word of God to come alive in my personal life. I was that deer in Psalm 8: 1a: "As the deer pants for the living waters, so my soul longs after you, O Lord." After five years of living in exile in the United States of America, while leading the Miracle Women Workshops; I experienced the call to ordained ministry. I initially refused that call because I was waiting for the war to end and my life to return to normalcy. I was also waiting for my husband to join us in America permanently or for the children and me to return to Liberia permanently.

From May 1990 until September 1995 I lived in a kind of limbo. I was hoping for a sign that I would get my old life back. I am so grateful for my pastor, Bishop Vashti Murphy McKenzie, who saw all that was unfolding in me, helped me understand my leadership abilities and spent time training and mentoring me. It became apparent to everyone that God was moving me in the direction of church leadership. I preached my first sermon on December 20, 1995, and became a Licentiate (licensed preacher). I was then given the title Minister to Women at Payne Memorial AME Church. All through those years, while I waited for the fullness of God's divine plan for my life, I was given opportunities to learn, to grow and to lead.

Since December 22, 1995, the ministry has placed me on a fast, convoluted road. In 1996, God compelled me to go to the refugee camps in Ghana to minister to displaced women and children through the Love Baton Project. From that trip, the Miracle Women Worldwide Ministries, Inc. (MWWM) was established. In 1997, I made a mission trip to Liberia. I took Love Batons and held a 3-day Spiritual and Economic Empowerment Revival. This birthed the Liberian branch of MWWM. When I returned in 1999, MWWM, Liberia was an ecumenical ministry comprising of over fifty women from seven Christian denominations.

In 2001, I returned to my home Liberia and established the Empowerment Temple A.M.E. Church. In 2008, I felt the prophetic call to Episcopal Leadership, and I began to pray diligently for God's direction. Once I acknowledged that call; I became anxious as to the timing to make the big announcement. The Holy Spirit held me back as a mother would grab the hand of a child who impetuously runs to cross the street without looking carefully in both directions for moving vehicles. While waiting for the manifestation of that calling; the opportunity came for me to enroll in the Doctor of Ministry Program (DMin) as a Beeson Scholar at Asbury Theological Seminary in Wilmore, Kentucky. I completed the program, graduating (first female from Africa) with the distinction of Most Distinguished Dissertation for Pastoral Leadership Award.

I was still waiting for God's permission to begin the journey to episcopal leadership. In 2012, after obtaining the DMin degree, the Holy Spirit spoke: "The time is now. You can announce your candidacy and offer yourself for episcopal service."

I had been waiting since 2008. During that time up until the present, I have navigated several leadership paths. These paths have included the following positions.

- Vice-president of the Connectional Women in Ministry
- Vice-president for the second largest undergraduate university in Liberia
- chairing the Global Leadership Summit which facilitates leadership development summits across the nation of Liberia
- serving the Supreme Court of Liberia as the first and only female clergy on the Grievance and Ethics Commission
- chairing the Board of Examiners of the Central Liberia Annual Conference
- serving as the President of the Board of Directors of the Central Liberia Annual Conference

- establishing the NGO, Helping Our People Excel, Inc.

On March 30, 2014, Liberia was hit by the Ebola Virus Epidemic that killed over 4000 men, women, and children. Bishop Clement W. Fugh was the assigned Bishop to the 14th Episcopal District at that time. The next series of Annual Conferences across the district were scheduled for February to May 2015. The Ebola epidemic was not yet over. Due to travel restrictions imposed by the United States of America, Bishop Fugh, an American citizen, was constrained to remain in America. The 14th Episcopal District covers the nations: Liberia, Sierra Leone, Ghana, Nigeria, Cote d'Ivoire, Benin, and Togo. The Ebola virus massively hit Liberia and Sierra Leone. Nigeria had a few deaths, and the remaining five countries were under serious threat. In the 14th District, there is a unique provision for the preservation and continuity of leadership in the absence of episcopal leaders because of war or other disasters. It is called the Board of Directors. (Doctrine and Discipline of the AME Church 2016, 306-308).

Bishop Fugh asked me to fulfill that provision by presiding over the 7th Session of the Central Liberia Annual Conference convened in April 2015. I could not believe that the Bishop would trust his conference to me. Bishop Fugh was quick to assure me that he had full confidence in my abilities. Secondly, I was very concerned that the election of delegates to the General Conference would be conducted without problems. Bishop Fugh provided guidelines and reminded me to follow the Doctrine and Discipline of the AME Church to the letter. Thirdly, I

wondered if the members of the conference would coop-
erate with me and respectfully allow me to stand in the
shoes of the Bishop to conduct the affairs of the annual
conference. I am pleased to report that the annual conference went very well, all of its business was executed cor-
rectly, and the election of delegates went smoothly without
judicial challenge. It is an experience I will never forget.

<u>David's Story</u>

David was the youngest of Jesse's eight sons. While
his brothers served as great soldiers in the Israeli army,
winning battles against the Philistines; David stayed at
home tending to the family sheep. He was probably well
loved and protected because of his young age. However,
scripture describes him as very strong and brave having
killed lions and bears who were a danger to the sheep.
(1 Samuel 17: 34-37). At a time when King Saul had
fallen out of favor with Jehovah; the prophet Samuel is
instructed to go to the house of Jesse and anoint one
of his sons to be the new king of Israel. Jesse presents
his strong older sons who are all rejected by the prophet
Samuel. Finally, Prophet Samuel asks if those were all
the sons wherein Jesse replied that there is one more, but
he is out tending the sheep. David is sent for, and immediately Samuel is prompted by the spirit of the Lord to
anoint the shepherd boy David as the new King of Israel.

Instead of immediately assuming power, many years
would pass before David sits on the throne as king over
all of the tribes of Israel. (2 Samuel 5). During the frustrating years of waiting, David serves in the king's palace

as a harpist. He accepts Goliath's challenge and he kills the giant. David becomes a refugee living in caves, and a mercenary with a band of fighters. To save his life, David is constrained to pretend to be crazy. To win the hand of Micah, King Saul's daughter, David kills thousands of Philistines. He went through all of this, yet he would be denied his seat on the throne for many years. Banned by King Saul and labeled a 'wanted man'; David would know no peace. He was targeted for death just because God chose him to be the leader. The people loved him, but King Saul hated him, was intimidated by him and jealous of him.

Scripture reports that David had two opportunities to kill Saul, an act that would remove the obstacle to his ascension to leadership of Israel. In I Samuel 24: 3-7, David comes upon Saul as he is resting in a cave unprotected. Instead of killing him, David cuts a piece of Saul's royal robe but leaves him unharmed. The second incident is recorded in I Samuel 26: 5-20. Again, David comes upon a sleeping Saul. Instead of killing him, he takes away Saul's spear and water jug.

In each case, David teaches us that leadership is about God's timing and not just about opportunity. David submitted himself to four evolutionary phases before finally serving as the King of Israel.

1. The Time of Anointing
2. The Time of Preparation
3. The Time of Persecution
4. The Time of Enthronement

Lessons Learned

Many of us remember the insistent call of God and the pull of the Holy Spirit to go into ministry or to lead in a specific area in our communities. Others affirm that call, recognizing the gifts in us and yet we are still waiting for the appointment, the ordination or the consecration. David was familiar with the pain of knowing where one's destiny is and being continually denied of reaching it.

I announced my candidacy for episcopal service in 2012 but was unsuccessful in my bid for election in 2016. Losing was, to say the least, very painful. Some of you reading this have had this experience. However, the pain of defeat and rejection must be acknowledged. It should never be masked by a façade of super strength and sto- icism. However, we must not succumb to anger, frustra- tion, discouragement, and fatigue. On my first Sunday after returning from the General Conference 2016; I stood before the congregation of Empowerment Temple AME Church. I had asked the Holy Spirit to give me a word of healing for the people and for myself. The sermon asked the question "Can You Still Trust God?" from Job 2:9-10. The Lord had spoken clearly in my heart that God is trust- worthy and that the quest for episcopal leadership can be trusted to God. I told the members of Empowerment Temple that we should not be like Job's wife and curse God and kill the vision.

A good friend was very concerned and asked me why I am again going through all the stress of campaigning to be a bishop when I am already serving well in ministry. I replied that being a bishop allows me to stand in a place of increased leverage for global impact for the kingdom of God and the advancement of my beloved AME Church. I desire to continue to serve well and strong but to help more people and impact greater change in this world and in my church. Where you stand determines the scope of your view and the dimensions of your reach.

We are tempted to enter into self-doubt, fatalistic resignation, anger, cynicism, and inactivity when our plans are thwarted. Resist it. Instead, use that time to seek for other ways to utilize your leadership gifts and broaden your experience. Use that time to explore new ways to lead and to embark on side trips in leadership. This book would probably still be an unfinished project if I had not used this period to focus and complete it.

I would never have sharpened the art of leadership development if I had only stayed in the area of pastoral leadership. I would have never gained valuable knowledge of the legal system if I had not accepted to serve on the Grievance and Ethics Commission of the Supreme Court of Liberia. I would never have learned the art of administration in higher education if I had not accepted the position of Vice President of a University. I would have never mentored doctoral students to a successful dissertation if I had not agreed to be a dissertation coach at Asbury Theological Seminary. If I had opted to remain inactive from the year when I first heard the call (2008); I would have missed all of these leadership opportunities and experiences. The Lord gives the vision, but it is for an appointed time. While we wait, we must still lead. It is selfish for us to withhold sharing our God-given gifts and training while we fix our eyes on a higher calling or a more prominent position.

David gave us the example. He led by being an excellent shepherd; caring and protecting his father's sheep. Even after prophet Samuel anointed him, David went back to his shepherd's work. He led the Israeli army to victory by killing Goliath. Even while he was mocked by his brothers and labeled a fool; he still rose up with sling and stones to face Goliath. He led his Mighty Men to fight successful battles against the Philistines. Even while a fugitive on the run from King Saul; he collaborated with Jonathan and others to protect Israel from the Philistines.

David understood that anointing precedes appointment. The anointing is an act of God's favor and being set aside for service. The time of preparation is when you build courage and acquire skills for leadership. David conquered Goliath, and this brought him into the palace to learn the ways of the king. David endured many persecutions at the hand of King Saul and those who wanted him dead. David remained firmly committed to obeying God, and he trusted God throughout those times. King Saul had to die for King David to be elevated. It may not be the physical death of a person, but it may be the death of an ideology and the birth of a new way of thinking. It may be the death of an era and the beginning of a new one. It may be the death of one generation and the birth of a new generation of leadership. It may require time for the people to prepare to venture into unexplored territory. The time of enthronement comes no matter the wait. David waited, and at God's appointed time David was crowned King of all of Israel.

The 51st Session of the AME General Conference convenes in 2020. I have, again, announced my candidacy for episcopal service. Daily, I am praying and working towards election as a bishop. I am telling my life and ministry story to the church whenever I have the opportunity to do so. I believe 2020 is God's timing for me to begin my service as a bishop to God's people in Africa. While I wait, I have purposed in my heart to continue to lead vigorously, creatively and passionately just where I am. Ecclesiastes 3:1 & 11a says: "There is an appointed time for everything. And there is a time for every event under heaven. He has made everything appropriate in its time..."(NASB)

Reflection and Response

You may have heard the compelling call of God to rise to a higher level of leadership. Yet, you feel you have failed because you were not elected, selected or appointed at the time you expected. Have you given up on your leadership quest? If not, what are you doing while you wait? How are you spending your days? What leadership opportunities have you ignored or thought insignificant because you are waiting for the big dream to come true? I want to encourage you to embrace all of life's experiences. I implore you to resist disillusionment and seize other leadership prospects. This is a journey to a destination. There are wonderful life lessons along the path. Like a tree, you can sprout leadership branches in so many different directions. Keep your eyes and mind open to opportunities._

Remember Jeremiah 29:11 & 14: "'For I know the plans that I have for you,' declares the Lord, 'plans for welfare and not for calamity to give you a future and a hope. I will be found by you,' declares the Lord, 'and I will restore your fortunes and will gather you from all the nations and from all the places where I have driven you,' declares the Lord, 'and I will bring you back to the place from where I sent you into exile.'".

Keep pressing forward and lead while you wait!!

<u>What's Your Story</u>

Journal

EPILOGUE

I have always felt that a story is not over though I have read the last words on the final page and closed the book. Neither is a movie over when I see the words 'The End" and the credits begin to roll. If the book or the movie was worth my time, then it will leave me wondering. I walk out of the theatre, and I close the book wanting to quench my wondering spirit. What if this or that had happened? Were all the issues resolved? Could the ending have been better, more exciting or less painful? I guess that is why writers of fiction are prompted to write sequels, and we buy tickets to go and see part two of a good movie.

You Can Lead! is non-fiction so we should close the last chapter of this book and move on. But as long as we live in human time and space, we keep producing life stories. We cannot change the facts of our lives or like a griot create multiple endings for a story depending on the audience; but, each day we add to our story or begin a new one.

As I carefully chose each story to include in this book, I realized that they did not just represent an incident in my life, but each story set me wondering: Why? What Next? This prompted me to examine my journey more closely to find meaningful connections with God's divine leading in my life. The 'wondering' exposed the steady hand of God nudging and guiding me on to success even through events that could have destroyed me. The 'wondering' caused me to align biblical stories with my stories and find spiritual insight to lighten the path to self-discovery.

"I looked for someone among them who would build up the wall and stand before me in the gap on behalf of the land so I would not have to destroy it, but I found none." (Ezekiel 22:30).

In the past, I would read this scripture and feel depressed. The idea that there may be no one to fill a leadership gap, no matter the size of the gap, made me despair for our families, our communities, our nations, the Church, the world. My melancholy dissipates as my stories reveal the times I have stepped forward to fill a leadership gap.

I encourage you to allow yourself to embrace your stories fully, no matter how painful or how pleasurable. With God's help, you must find the courage to tackle the What Next question. It is when you reflect on the What Next; then you will realize that it has always been God's spirit right there with you all along guiding you to unique paths for fulfilling your leadership potential.

You may appear to be born in the 'wrong' country, on the 'wrong' continent, living in the 'wrong' neighborhood, with the 'wrong' skin color, named and treated as the 'weaker' vessel, and with no academic letters to the right of your last name. But you are alive, and you have your story, and it's the 'right' story. Hopefully, while reading this book, you wrote down a couple of them. *You Can Lead!* made me realize that you may be part of a vast global army of gap-fillers who are sitting out there on the fringes and the back rows of society. Each of you has the potential to lead. What's Next?

Works Cited/Consulted

Augsburger, David W. *Conflict Mediation across Cultures.* Louisville: Westminster-John Knox, 1992.

Belin, Roderick D. *"The Doctrine and Discipline of the African Methodist Episcopal Church 2016".* Nashville, Tenn. The AME Sunday School Union, 2017.

Bruggeman, Walter. *Interpretation: First and Second Samuel.* Louisville: John Knox, 1990.

Burns, James MacGregor. *Leadership.* New York: Harper Perennial, 1982.

Cho, Kiusk. "Do Women Lead Differently? Leadership Styles of Top Women Leaders." *Building Leadership Bridges.* Ed. Cynthia Cherry, Larrain R. Matusak, and Shelly Wilsey. College Park, MD: MacGregor Burns Academy, 2001. 32-44.

Cooper, Katurah. "A Calling Out of War and Guns." *Women in the Ministry: Their Trials and Their Triumphs.* Ed. Mahlangu-Ngcobo Mankekolo. Baltimore, MD: Gateway, 2000. 37-43.

Gbowee, Leymah. *And Mighty Be Our Powers*. New York: Beast, 2011.

Hack, Nadine. "Liberia: Women's Mass Action for Peace and 'Pray the Devil Back to Hell' screening at Samuel K. Doe Stadium." *AllAfrica.com*. 9 Mar. 2012. 26 Apr. 2012 <http://allafrica.com/stories/200903170823.html>.

Hughes, Richard L., Robert C. Ginnet, and Gordon J. Curphy. *Leadership: Enhancing the Lessons of Experience*. New York: McGraw, 2009.

Johnson-Sirleaf, Ellen. *This Child Will Be Great*. New York: Harper, 2009.

Liberia National Elections Commission. *Results of 2005 Elections* Press release. Monrovia. 23 Nov. 2005.

"Liberia's Uneasy Peace." *Online News Hour*. Public Broadcasting System. 25 Jan. 2011 <www.pbs.org/newshour/bb/africa/liberia/post1980_timeline.html>.

McKenzie, Vashti Murphy. *Journey to the Well*. New York: Penguin Compass, 2002.

_____.*Swapping Housewives: Rachel and Jacob and Leah*. Cleveland: The Pilgrim Press, 2007.

Meyers, Carol, Tony Craven, and Ross S. Kraemer, Editors. *Women in Scripture: A Dictionary of Named and Unnamed Women in the Hebrew Bible, the Apocryphal/Deuterocanonical Books, and the New Testament*. Boston: Houghton, 2000.

Nouwen, Henri J. M. *The Wounded Healer*. New York: Doubleday Image Books, 1990.

Nwoye, Miriam Agatha Chinwe. "Role of Women in Peace Building and Conflict Resolution in African Traditional Societies: A Selective Review." Paper presented at

Kenyatta U, Nairobi, Kenya. 12 Dec. 2010 <http://www.afrikaworld.net/ afrel/chinwenwoye.htm>.

Oduyoye Mercy A., Musimbi, R.A. Kanyoro, Editors. *The Will to Arise: Women, Tradition and the Church in Africa.* New York: Orbis Books, 1992.

Ogbonna-Nwaogu, Ifeyinwa Maureen. "Civil Wars in Africa: A Gender Perspective of the Cost on Women." *Journal of Social Science* 16 (2008): 251-58.

Seamands, Stephen. *Wounds That Heal.* Downers Grove, IL: InterVarsity, 2003.

Sorenson, Georgia, and Gill R. Hickman. "Invisible Leadership: Acting on Behalf of a Common Purpose." *Building Leadership Bridges.* Ed. Cynthia Cherry and Larrain R. Matusak. College Park, MD: MacGregor Burns Academy of Leadership, 2002. 7-24.

Steady, Filomina Chioma. *Women and Collective Action in Africa.* New York, N.Y.: Palgrave Macmillan, 2006.

WANEP Annual Report. Accra, Ghana: WANEP, 2003.

Watley, William D. *Roots of Resistance: The Nonviolent Ethic of Martin Luther King, Jr.* Valley Forge, PA: Judson, 1985.

Weem, Renita J. *Battered Love: Marriage, Sex and Violence in the Hebrew Prophets.* Minneapolis: Augsburg Fortress, 1995.

CPSIA information can be obtained
at www.ICGtesting.com
Printed in the USA
LVHW050049200820
663704LV00015B/427

9 781545 659182